WILD AT HOME

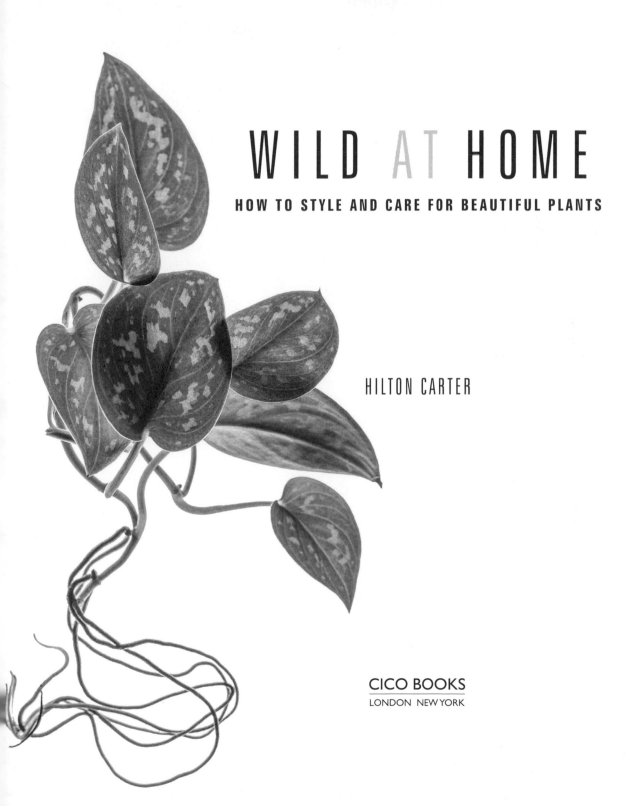

WILD AT HOME

HOW TO STYLE AND CARE FOR BEAUTIFUL PLANTS

HILTON CARTER

CICO BOOKS
LONDON NEW YORK

Published in 2019 by CICO Books
An imprint of Ryland Peters & Small Ltd

20–21 Jockey's Fields   341 E 116th St
London WC1R 4BW   New York, NY 10029

www.rylandpeters.com

10 9 8 7 6 5 4 3 2

A CIP catalog record for this book is available from the
Library of Congress and the British Library.

ISBN: 978-1-78249-713-4

Printed in China

Editor: Caroline West
Designer: Elizabeth Healey
Photographer: Hilton Carter

In-house editor: Anna Galkina
Art director: Sally Powell
Production controller: David Hearn
Publishing manager: Penny Craig
Publisher: Cindy Richards

contents

A peek through the greenery—as if walking through a jungle and stumbling upon a campsite. The bedroom at my studio, Jungle by the Falls, was designed with only one thought in mind... more sleep.

INTRODUCTION—INTO THE WILD

I was once told that if you follow your passion, regardless of what it is, you'll find your happiness. For me, this has meant creating a home with my wife, Fiona, which blurs the line between interior and exterior so seamlessly that the look just feels completely natural. Of course, I'm referring to the greenery that ties our home and studio together like a bow placed on a gift. From end to end, the theme of indoor jungle is ever-present and a mixed palette of greens sets the tone. Taking a step back, it's the greenery that binds together each room in our home and creates the feeling of tranquility throughout. It is achieving this sense of calm and peace that has motivated me to surround myself with foliage for the past five years and also the reason I wanted to create this book.

Whether this book is the first of many or the only one, I can't even begin to express how much it means to me. *Wild at Home* feels as if I'm giving the reader a peek into my personal diary. It contains my thoughts, tips, and a few of my secrets for styling plants and how best to care for them. Never in my wildest dreams did I

think I would write a book like this. My passion for greenery is uncontrollable and, because of the natural trial and error I've gone through, I've always felt that it was only right for me to share my knowledge with others who might be going through the same issues I have had in the past. For me, sharing with others in this "green" community, which seems to be growing every day, inspires me to be a better plant parent and I hope it does the same for them too.

Over the past five years, I've developed many imaginative methods for bringing greenery into my home, while also styling the plants in such a way that they impart a beautiful energy to the space. I share many of these methods within the pages of this book. I have helped some of my friends to transform their living spaces with plants, and their homes are also showcased in the book. From important decisions as to which types of plants work best in a particular setting to creative suggestions for the base trays to use beneath pots, there will be something in this book to make you think differently about the way you style your home and your greenery.

HOW I GOT STARTED:
FRANK, MY FIDDLE-LEAF FIG

Whenever anyone asks if I have a favorite plant in my collection, I never hesitate to say Frank, my fiddle-leaf fig. Frank was the first major plant purchase I ever made and marked the start of my plant obsession. I was living in the French Quarter of New Orleans. One of the reasons I moved into my apartment there was the floor-to-ceiling windows that looked out onto the street below. I wasn't into the idea of using shades or drapes (curtains) to cover the windows for a bit of privacy. So, I decided to use a few plants to do this instead. When I purchased Frank in the spring of 2014, it seemed as if *Ficus lyrata*, the fiddle-leaf fig, was the "it" plant for interior designers and stylists. You would see them in magazines and movies, and on TV shows, etc. But it wasn't its popularity that made the fiddle-leaf fig catch my eye, but rather the shape, texture, and color of the foliage that instantly drew me in. I was also looking for something more tree-shaped and this particular fiddle was just that. When you're at a nursery, you'll notice that fiddles come in a few different shapes. You'll find fiddles with one long branch; fiddles made of a few long branches, which gives them a more bushy look; and others, like Frank, that started as one branch and were then split into many branches, to produce a tree-like shape.

When I got Frank home, I did not know how to care for a fiddle-leaf fig, other than to supply good light and water. I just happened to luck out in having a space with a lot of great light throughout the day and which was humid enough for Frank's watering needs to stay consistent. I placed Frank in front of one of the large windows in my living room and for a year he thrived and grew larger. Clusters of three new leaves would grow from one branch and then the other, like clockwork.

OPPOSITE
Cleaning Frank, my fiddle-leaf fig, in my living-room window.

That first spring and summer made me think I really knew what I was doing. It wasn't until a year later, when I moved into a new apartment which wasn't as bright that I first started to become a better plant parent. You see, it took for Frank's leaves to start getting brown spots or turn yellow and fall off for me to really focus on what was required to keep him alive. When everything was going great and Frank was thriving, I had no need to learn more about what a fiddle requires, because I had just stumbled on the right setting for him. But it's when you are struggling with a specimen that your plant parenting is truly tested. I was told that fiddles don't like being moved and here I was witnessing this firsthand. Not only had I moved from a space with amazing light and high ceilings to one with hardly any light and low ceilings, I then only stayed in the new apartment for three months before moving Frank again. And this time he had to get packed up in the back of a dark moving truck and driven 1,100 miles from New Orleans to Baltimore.

A view of the bedroom corner at my studio, Jungle by the Falls (JBTF). The chaise longue was the first piece I placed there. The window is framed by *Strelitzia reginae* (bird of paradise), with its paddle-like leaves, on the left, and *Livistona chinensis* (Chinese fan palm), on the right.

So many of you fear bringing plants such as Frank into your home, either because you've been unsuccessful in the past or have heard how hard they are to keep alive. Also, the cost of buying indoor plants nowadays is enough to make anyone think twice before purchasing them. But let me hold your hand through this process. There are a few things I've learned about caring for my fiddles and other plants, so I hope the advice I give in *Plant-care Essentials* (see pages 94–141) will help guide you in caring for your own indoor plants, too. Remember, we are a community and all in this together. So, I got your back!

ABOVE
Our cat, Isabella, loves to hide out in the greenery.

RIGHT
Fiona watering the hanging plants in the bedroom at JBTF.

chapter one

green in the home

Without plants in my life, I'm not
sure how I'd find a good moment
to let down my hair, take it all in,
and breathe

A LOVE LETTER TO GREENERY

roses are red, violets are blue, but what about all the wonderful greens? It's always been the color—as much as the shape—of foliage that has attracted me. From the deep, stark greens of *Ficus lyrata* (fiddle-leaf fig) to the burgundy that penetrates the new growth of *Philodendron* 'Rojo Congo', there is a wide variety of greenery that can turn a simple space into a lush oasis.

Have you ever seen a variegated monstera? The way in which the green and white come together like a piece of marble cake is perfection. It's these small nuances that can make a home vibrate—and you with it. For instance, if you look more closely at a specimen of *Ficus elastica* (rubber plant) and examine its lines properly, you'll notice that the leaves have a thin, vibrant red stroke, which, when seen at the right moment and in the right light, can look neon. The saying "don't judge a book by its cover" is clearly true in the case of the rubber plant. Judge if you wish, but you'll likely come to the same conclusion—"Wow."

For me, the beauty that exists in plants from a visual perspective is just the first reason why I bring them into my home. The fact that they can transform a living space immediately is the next. An indoor jungle embodies all the wild uniqueness of a real outdoor jungle. *Strelitzia reginae* (bird of paradise), for example, can grow to a height of about 20 feet (6m) in a space where the light is right, and the resulting vibe of the space is then basically dictated by the powerful presence of that plant. Greenery sets the tone. But I think what makes all the time and stress that goes into caring for this sort of vibe worthwhile is how wonderful it makes you feel. Have you ever been trapped indoors, for whatever reason, then stepped outside and experienced that moment when the first blast of fresh air hits the back of your nostrils? Well, that feeling can be replicated almost daily at home if you have plants.

It is certainly the green in my home that I thank for calming me down when life's weight wants to sit on my shoulders. It's in my indoor jungle that I find escape and shelter. There's no question that the person who thought up the term "staycation" must have had plants at home. In my home, getting snowed in is a welcome inconvenience, what you might call a good problem to have. Because, regardless of what the weather is doing outside, the greenery indoors makes my wife and me feel as if we're sitting below a tree canopy in the tropics.

In short, I've seen my love for plants grow, from that very first moment when the seed of my passion for greenery was sown to its blossoming in the present day. My love for greenery has continued to bloom and also connected me with a like-minded community across the globe in so many interesting ways. I've enjoyed every moment of it.

OPPOSITE, TOP

A gallery wall of art and greenery is a must-have. Using a mirror as an air-plant holder or propagating large cuttings of *Philodendron* 'Burle Marx' in vases are two plant-styling techniques that can make a space stand out.

FRIENDS WITH BENEFITS

a s a kid I never went camping. Honestly, even if the opportunity had arisen, I'm not sure I would have jumped at it. I didn't understand the desire to sleep outdoors on the cold ground, dig holes to relieve myself, and create fire with sticks and stones. Where I was from, this was what the homeless did because that was their only way to survive, and I for one loved the benefits of living in a house. Now,

Scindapsus pictus 'Argyraeus'

as an adult, I can understand the desire much better. But, don't get me wrong, I still don't go camping. Instead, I got creative and designed a space where I could bring the outside in. I figured out how to get the best of both worlds. What I do might be regarded as low-key "glamping." To me, having plants is like camping, but with all the benefits of never leaving the house (Netflix, a toilet, no bugs, and best of all, your own bed). Actually, I need to make a correction here. You may see a bug or two. Who am I kidding? When I said I've brought the outside in, that's exactly what I meant. And the benefits of doing so far outweigh the possibility of a gnat or two here and there.

Bringing greenery into your home has so many positive benefits. For me, not only are you creating a space that can artfully blur the line between interior and exterior, but also one that has great depth. This depth is warm and inviting, and at the end of the day brings a real sense of euphoria. You are literally giving your space life and turning what was just a house into a home. You create a kind of true connection, as if you are at one with nature again.

Have you ever walked into a plant nursery or greenhouse and instantly felt a change in the air? The feeling of calm that washes over you as you tilt your head back, close your eyes, and take in a deep breath. This is the feeling you're looking to replicate when you bring plants into your home. And, honestly, you'll be doing yourself a disservice if you don't try to do this.

BOTTOM RIGHT
Use mirrors to show off another view or corner from a different perspective. This view of one corner of my living room shows a *Ravenea rivularis* (majestic palm).

Beyond the uplifting feeling they give, plants also have so many health-enhancing properties. Not only do they improve the air quality and oxygen levels in your home, but they also help to raise the humidity level, which can be good for your skin. Having plants in your bedroom is one of the smartest places you can keep them. Tonight, try nestling up to a *Sansevieria trifasciata* (snake plant). It will improve the air quality in your bedroom, continually giving off oxygen and taking in all the carbon dioxide you breathe out while sleeping. Can you say the same for your partner or spouse? I didn't think so. Another great bedroom bud is *Epipremnum aureum* (golden pothos), often known as devil's ivy. The golden pothos can be encouraged to creep along the walls of your room, which not only looks cool, but also helps purify the air while you sleep.

Lastly, the greatest benefit provided by plants, in my opinion, is the sense of pride you feel in caring for them well. There's something so special about knowing you are the reason a plant thrives and flourishes. You start to have a maternal/paternal feeling toward your plants that really makes you zone in on them. Personally, I see the time I spend watering plants as my moment to meditate. I set the mood and completely "zen out." Without plants in my life, I'm not sure how I'd find a good moment to let down my hair, take it all in, and breathe.

Bringing greenery into your home has so many positive benefits. For me, not only are you creating a space that can artfully blur the line between interior and exterior, but also one that has great depth.

SHOPPING FOR PLANTS

going shopping for plants should be something you get really excited about. In my case, you don't accumulate over 300 plants without finding joy in shopping for them—bringing in fresh greenery always brightens up my day. Make sure you turn it into a fun experience for yourself, too. Getting worried and stressed is not the right way to go about it. When you're a novice plant enthusiast, knowing the best way to shop will save you time, money, and, ultimately, a whole lot of stress. It will also make a world of difference to how successful you will be.

Although many websites offer to ship a plant to you on the same day, the idea of shopping for plants online just isn't for me. I like to be in the nursery and have the advantage of seeing each plant I buy—I like to have my eyes on it and my hands in it. Being with a plant in this way helps you better understand its size and shape, and visualize where you might see it going in your home. When you shop online—and let's just say, for example, that you're looking to order a *Monstera deliciosa* (Swiss cheese plant)—you don't know exactly what monstera you'll get; you're just going to receive whichever monstera the supplier decides to send you. I want to be the one making that choice, just as if I were adopting a new puppy. Just as all puppies from the same litter aren't identical, so no one plant is the same as another. I want to be the one doing the choosing. This part of the process is such an important factor in whether you will be successful in keeping your plant alive. For me to give you advice on caring for and styling with plants, I feel it's important that you first understand how to go about shopping for them. At the end of the day, the more you know about plant shopping upfront, the better off you'll be in the end. So, with that said, here are my steps for successful plant shopping.

OPPOSITE
Shopping for plants at Terrain, a garden-supply store in Glen Mills, Pennsylvania, is one of my favorite things to do.

The
Earth Fired Clay
COLLECTION

OPPOSITE

The pots at Terrain are some of
my favorites for using at home.

1 **HOW MUCH LIGHT DO YOU HAVE?** First things first, before you even leave home, decide on the spot where you want to place a plant. Take a note of the amount of light that spot receives. This will determine which plant or plants you can bring into that space. Let's say you notice that your home is only made up of dark corners, but you've been inspired by all the examples of *Ficus lyrata* (fiddle-leaf fig) you've seen styled in other people's homes, perhaps via the Internet, and think you'd like that look too. Well, sorry to be the bearer of bad news, but you don't have enough light to keep a fiddle-leaf fig alive. So, for you, the best plants would be *Zamioculcas zamiifolia* (fern arum/ZZ plant), *Calathea lancifolia* (rattlesnake plant), *Spathiphyllum wallisii* (peace lily), and possibly as many specimens of *Sansevieria trifasciata* (snake plant) as your heart desires.

2 **ASK FOR ADVICE AT THE NURSERY** Once you've assessed the type of light in each area of your home where you'd like to place a plant, take that information to the nursery. Find an assistant and ask as many questions as you like. Assistants at most nurseries are usually very well versed in the plants they have at that particular location. Tell them exactly what type of light you have and they will be able to advise you which plants are best suited to your home.

3 TAKE IDENTIFICATION PICTURES After looking over all the options, make sure to take a picture of the label or sign that tells you exactly what that plant is (in case you can't remember the name later). Most nurseries have signage for all the types of plants they have and also a few tips on how to care for them. If there isn't any signage on the plants, or labels or tags, ask one of the assistants and write that information down. Knowing what type of plant you have can make all the difference. It will save you a lot of time and stress because you will know exactly what questions to ask and what to look up when a particular plant begins taking a turn or shows signs that you feel aren't right.

4 CHECK YOUR PLANT CAREFULLY Once you've decided on a plant, check for any bugs that might be hiding, hoping to take a ride back to your home. Check on top of and underneath the leaves, and make sure you also check around the edges of the potting mix. Bugs are part of nature and having plants in your home, but if you can avoid bringing in unwanted critters, why not start at the nursery?

5 FIND A SUITABLE POT Now it's time to find the right pot for your plant. Firstly, you need to make sure that the new pot is at least 2 inches (5cm) larger in diameter then the nursery pot. Try this out by placing the plant inside the new pot and assessing how it looks. Once you've found the right pot, make sure you also grab a base tray (see page 35). This is essential if you have a planter with a drainage hole. Personally, I prefer to put my plants in pots with drainage holes.

6 CHOOSE THE RIGHT POTTING MIX You need to ensure you get the right potting mix for that particular type of plant. Again, if you're in any doubt what type of potting mix is required, ask an assistant at the nursery. If you're planning to grow a plant in a pot without a drainage hole, you will need to buy some small stones and horticultural charcoal, as well as fresh potting mix, to create a buffer and prevent waterlogging (see page 103). Make sure you ask someone about this as well.

TOOLS OF THE TRADE

apron

For me, wearing an apron while caring for plants is basically the same as a carpenter or craftsman wearing a tool-belt. It allows you to have all the necessary tools readily available—not to mention that it keeps you a bit dry when watering a thousand plants. Okay, so maybe I'm exaggerating, but if you're spending hours every week watering plants, then you might want to invest in an apron. I had the one shown below custom-made to fit the particular tools I like to carry when caring for my plant buds. Take note of the pocket for my phone. I asked for that addition because you never know what you might want to capture when you're at the top of a ladder.

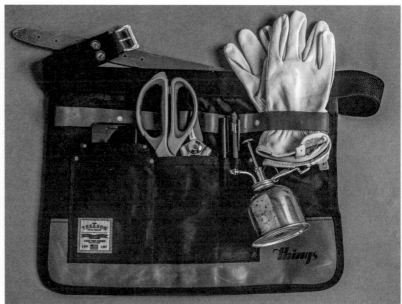

watering can

A watering can is the staple tool for a plant parent or enthusiast. How else can you provide the water—and nutrients if you're using a dilute liquid feed—that your plants need? You can't just carry water over with your hands! Over the past few years, I've become a collector of beautifully designed but functional watering cans. I figured that if I have to spend three to four hours some days watering plants, I might as well look good while I'm doing it. There are so many different types of watering cans out there: ceramic, metal, and plastic varieties—many of them unique and well designed. If you're going to invest in a large expensive plant, why not invest in a nice watering can too? If you don't, it's like having a lovely set of dinnerware, but eating with plastic forks. My search for the perfect watering can led me to designing one made from ceramic, as I was tired of tin cans rusting over time and not working as well. Plus, plastic watering cans just aren't cool or attractive. So, I collaborated with two ceramic artist friends to create something that not only looks elegant and stylish, but also has the functionality to provide the perfect pour.

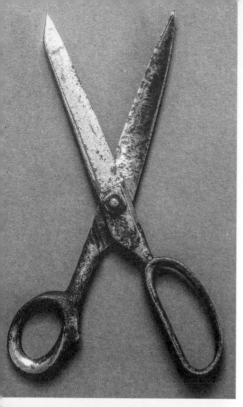

sharp objects

Having sharp pruning shears (secateurs), scissors, or even a blade is crucial when caring for your plants, as something to cut with is a huge part of the pruning process. A sharp instrument is also one of the major tools in propagating, as being able to make a very sharp cut is important. Nowadays, there are so many different styles of pruning shears that it's really hard to make a bad choice. I don't find it necessary to go out and spend $30–40 (£25–30) on shears just based on how they look when what's really important is finding something sharp. So, if you have a sharp pair of scissors and wish to use those, then so be it. It's all about the cut.

little spades

Most gardeners have a small gardening spade or digger in their tool kit. This allows you to dig deep into the potting mix to create a small hole for planting. A small spade is also helpful when you need to dig into the potting mix in order to remove a plant from its pot. It also allows you to scoop up the potting mix when potting or repotting a plant. I often find myself using an old vintage ice-cream spoon, as it is something I already have lying around and, honestly, it produces the same results. Indeed, I like to find ways to utilize what I already have at hand or items that bring a bit more style and individuality to what is already out there. So using an ice-cream spoon to scoop up potting mix or dig holes for repotting works just as well for me as any spade you'd find at a garden store. You just shouldn't use it again to scoop your ice cream.

Mr. Mister

Misting your plants throughout the week can help to raise the humidity in your home, which will also benefit your plants. Finding the right mister isn't easy, though. I use a small tin mister to spray succulents or air plants and a typical spray bottle for my ferns, fiddle-leaf fig, and *Strelitzia reginae* (bird of paradise) and other large tropical plants. For me, misting my plants is one of my favorite ways to relax. There's something so euphoric about the whole misting process.

The Cradle

While I agree that you can use just about any glass vessel for propagating your plant babies, I think "The Cradle," designed by yours truly, is the best and most stylish way to do so. I might be slightly biased here, but my Cradle, which is made from Maryland walnut wood, does the trick and does it well. You simply slot the glass vessels containing the cuttings into the holes and then either hang the cradle on a wall or sit it on top of a table or windowsill (see page 45 for a picture of our propagation wall composed of multiple cradles).

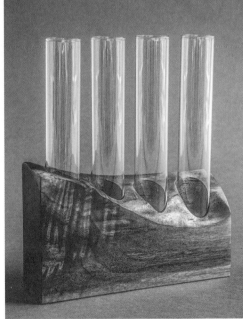

gloves

Let's just be clear: if you have plants, then you're going to have to get your hands dirty from time to time. That's just inevitable. However, you can limit that exposure by wearing gloves when potting up plants and definitely when you're handling cacti. I can't tell you the number of times I've found myself in a sticky situation when potting a cactus (pun intended) and made the mistake of not wearing gloves. So, fair warning, protect your hands when you can.

styling with plants

'I see incorporating plants as one of

the key requirements when designing

an interior space, just as much as a

couch or coffee table would be'

OPPOSITE

This group planting of *Cereus repandens* (Peruvian apple cactus) is sandwiched perfectly between the windows in my studio bedroom. A quick tip: I like adding mirrors to my spaces wherever possible to reflect light into dark corners. This mirror catches a little sun and scatters it toward the *Epipremnum aureum* (golden pothos), which can be seen in the reflection.

PLANTING BY DESIGN

a personal style is how we all show off our individuality to the world. The same approach should apply when introducing greenery into your home. What will make your space different from those of your friends and family? How do you create that "wow" factor? Bringing greenery into your home shouldn't be as simple as going to a nursery, grabbing the first plant you see, and then dropping it next to a window. However, the sad thing is that many believe this to be the case.

For me, I see incorporating plants as one of the key requirements when designing an interior space, just as much as a couch or coffee table would be. Let's break this down—the staples for a new home are a bed, a couch, a refrigerator, and a plant, and not necessarily in that order. I might be a bit biased here, but it's really that simple. The thing is, how do you go about purchasing the right couch for your home? Well, when you're couch shopping, you make decisions based on so many variables: the size of the space you have, the color, the texture, how comfortable it is, and so on. These are also all the things you should consider when purchasing a plant.

finding your statement plant

The main aim when styling a room is to find your statement piece or even better, your statement plant. This statement plant is the one that has a particular look and sets the overall tone and feel of the room. It's the one plant in a room that makes you or your guests take a moment to just stare and be fully taken by what's in front of them. This plant will ask—no, demand—immediate attention. For me, my choice of statement plant has been influenced by a need to bring in plants with a tree-like shape. Think about it, how many people do you know that literally have a tree in their home? I know, exactly. There really is something special about that. To me, that's what I call a statement. The statement plant introduces the "wow" factor because your guest will just stand there in awe and undoubtedly mouth, "Wow." And isn't that what all of us really want? To make our friends jealous of our plants? All joking aside, what you are really aiming to do—and what I personally take great joy in—is to leave your guests inspired. Your statement plant will undoubtedly be one that makes your guests leave your home wanting to have the same in theirs.

form, shape, and scale

Selecting your statement plant will obviously be based on personal preference, the level of care you can give, and the environment you have in your home (that is, how much light and space there is). Once you've figured all this out, you'll need to think about the form and size of the plant that will work best in your home. I find plants such as *Strelitzia reginae* (bird of paradise), *Ficus elastica* (rubber plant), different types of palms, and the *Ficus lyrata* (fiddle-leaf fig)

to be great choices for setting the tone or making that statement for you. The reason is simple. These plants can mature into really large specimens and live for generations. Beyond their overall size, however, the scale of their foliage is also crucial when transforming your home into an indoor jungle. The size of a bird of paradise leaf alone, for example, will immediately stop someone in their tracks.

The other reason why I love using plants such as these as a main feature is because they have shapes that work anywhere in a room without interrupting the flow. Given that most of them grow upward and outward, you don't have to worry about them taking up too much floor space. For example, if you place a fiddle-leaf fig by your bed, you won't be prevented from sleeping because of an invasive branch. As a result of its tree-like shape, the fig will grow above the bed, keeping the space below clear. You could achieve the same effect with similar tropical plants such as rubber plants and Swiss cheese plants—with each continuing that feeling of an indoor jungle throughout your home.

"dress" your plant

Now with all that said, you can't just place a naked plant in your home. Have some humanity, dammit! You have to make sure your plant has the right dress or slacks—in other words, you need to find the right pot as its base. This is a package deal, a partnership, if you will. So finding the right pot to match your plant matters—for more on this, see *Pots and Base Trays*, on the following pages.

FAR LEFT
A group of cacti sitting in the bedroom window of my studio.

LEFT
A selection of the terrariums you'll find at Terrain in Glen Mills, Pennsylvania.

BELOW
I like to group cacti and succulents together because they all need watering at the same time.

POTS AND BASE TRAYS

choosing the right pot

finding the right pot or planter is key when styling your home with plants. Making the right decision when choosing a pot is obviously important in terms of plant care, but is everything when it comes to styling. The pot is the way you "dress" your plant so it will fit within the scheme of your space. You can't just take this part of the process for granted. There should be a reason behind every decision when you're choosing which pots to use.

Along with the growing popularity of indoor plants, there has been an explosion in the different types and styles of planters on the market. Whether it's really cool designs sold by large brands or local ceramic makers, the options can be endless. I usually suggest going for what fits the mood and tone of your existing space—that is, the color palette and design— while also being very mindful of the cost. Given the current plant buzz, these pots aren't cheap. So when the pots are must-haves, then clearly you just make the purchase, but when you're working on a budget and need to find pots for the gang of plants you purchased over the weekend, I advise going thrift shopping or taking a trip to the local flea market. These places are a treasure trove of vintage planters and objects that can be transformed into pots. Although all these items might not have a drainage hole, this is nothing a drill can't handle.

The first thing I do to ensure that I purchase the right pot is to consider its size against the size of the plant. Once you have the right size pot for your plant, then it's all about the look. For example, I take into account the color of the pot in relation to the color of the surrounding furniture. There is also a decision to make regarding what material the pot is made from. For example, plastic and glazed pots hold more water and moisture, while terracotta pots release more moisture, letting the roots and potting mix breathe.

Picking out the right pot should be part of the fun of having plants. It's a simple way to complement the interior design of your space, but also a really big way to show off your personal taste.

base trays

When it comes to styling your plants in the perfect pots, the one thing that isn't always provided, or even an option, is a nice base tray. With pots that have drainage holes, the water has to drain into something and no one likes the look of those cheap plastic base trays around the home. That's a clear sign of a lack of attention and, most of all, style.

So what are the options, you might ask? Well, for one, if you grow plants in terracotta pots, more than likely there will be base trays to match each size of pot. But what happens when you purchase a really cool designer pot that doesn't have a base tray? This is when you have to get creative! Try and see the potential in things you've never thought to use as a base tray before. I like to visit thrift stores and look for vintage plates with a tall lip, or shop online for quiche dishes and platters that can be used as base trays. The aim is to be imaginative and see how you can repurpose something to suit your planting needs. How many stylish vintage plates or trays do you have in your cabinets that have just been sitting around collecting dust? Put that beauty to good use!

PLANT ACCORDINGLY

In the art world you often hear of the rule of thirds, which is used as a guide for composing a piece of art so it's perfectly balanced. This method ensures the viewer moves their eyes across the entire frame and sees the picture in full. When styling your home with plants, try to use this idea as your rule of thumb. Or, better yet, your rule of green thumb. Creating an indoor jungle isn't just about bringing in a lot of plants and placing them randomly throughout your home. There should be a reason behind the decisions you make regarding the plants you bring in and where you place them. Approaching plant styling in this way will benefit you, your space, and, most of all, your plants. There should be a method to your green madness. Or at least that is the way I try to see it when I style a room with plants. To start with, I always consider the light in a room and the types of plants that will thrive there. Once that decision has been made, I then use three design techniques to help me position the plants—these are using layers, grouping, and creating levels (my own rule of thirds in a way). I try to sprinkle in a little of all three because when we're talking about styling, we must plant accordingly.

LEFT

Allowing climbing plants to clamber over interior features takes a space to the next level. Here, a pothos climbs over the mirror above the bar cart in my living room.

using layers

Think of the way a group photo is taken. Based on height, the photographer places taller individuals to the back and then everyone gets smaller as you move closer to the front. This guarantees that everyone's face will be seen in the photo. The same goes for layering plants. Layering your plants in this way guarantees that each plant will get its time in the light, but also face time with you. You don't want to place a large plant right next to the window and then smaller ones behind it for the following reasons. Firstly, it would mean that you'd never get any real visual benefit from the smaller plants. Secondly, it would be difficult for you to get to those plants for watering and other care tasks. Let's just say you only have one window in your home and you're a really wonderful person, so you want to fill that window with plants. What you should do in this case is place the larger plant to one side of the window, so it's not blocking the window completely, and then stagger the smaller plants on the window ledge next to it. Not only is this a good look for your space and style, but also helpful for the wellbeing of your plants.

I also use the layering technique by making decisions based on plant foliage. There are so many different types of foliage in a range of colors, shapes, and sizes. Using these to create a particular feel in your home is a must. In my case, mixing these up is what helps create that "wow" factor. In my studio bedroom, for example, I decided to showcase this method of layering with my plant throne (see page 52). What makes this sitting area so nice is the interplay between the shape of the *Ficus lyrata* (fiddle-leaf fig), the large leaves of the *Strelitzia reginae* (bird of paradise), and the dramatic leaves of the *Livistona chinensis* (Chinese fan palm). These three plants have such different shapes and textures that, even though they play in the background, they instantly pop to the front. (See *Jungle by the Falls*, pages 56–61, for more on this plant-throne area.)

Layering is one of the motifs you'll notice throughout any space I style. I know what it does for my own home, and providing that information and guidance for others just makes sense.

grouping plants

Grouping plants is a good design technique, but can also be helpful from a practical point of view. Indeed, I find it extremely practical to place my plants in groups based on their care needs and type. When you group plants based on their care needs, it helps you manage your time more efficiently. For example, let's say you have a lot of plants and most of them are on an every seven days watering schedule, but ten of your plants are on an every three days schedule. Grouping the every three days plants together will make it easier for you to remember which plants require attention every three days and keep you from overlooking a plant or overwatering another one. This method is really useful when you leave town and place the care of your plants in the hands of someone else. Grouping plants according to their care requirements makes it easy to tell the person looking after them which groups need what, rather than the instructions being based on individual plants. For more guidance on this, see *Getting a Plant Sitter*, page 115.

Grouping plants according to type can be great fun and also visually appealing because it helps give your home a distinctive look and feel. In my home, for example, I decided to group most of our cacti and succulents in one window. Doing so not only makes it easier to water them, but it also gives the window such a warm appearance and brings another mood to our home. We've created a little desert indoors. I adopt the same approach with my tropical plants to create a real sense of jungle. Whenever I think of tropical plants I think of being on vacation, near a beach, under the sun, and free of all my worries. Why wouldn't I want that feeling in my home every day?

ABOVE

A view down the bright hallway of our home. This long hallway has three large windows, which keeps all the plants very happy.

creating levels

I think creating levels with plants in your home is a perfect demonstration of using the rule of thirds. Regarding your living space as a whole and using not only the floor space but also the tables, counters, and walls as plant stands brings uniqueness and individuality to your home. Viewing the center of a dining table as only suitable for an arrangement of flowers is limiting. If you have the necessary light, why not place a large potted tree in the center of your table? If you have the ceiling height, why not utilize the space above the table by hanging an oversized wreath made of nothing but air plants? The key here is to spread out the green love so that when you step back from it and take a look, the indoor jungle you were looking to create can be actualized. But, to do this, you have to get creative and not limit your options.

When I want to give a grouping of plants a fresh look, I like to create levels by stacking wooden boards or stone slabs to make platforms for my plants to sit on. In my desert window I used cutting boards to create different levels between the smaller plants. In my studio living room, I decided to create a different level by using two terracotta pots for a single plant. By stacking the pots—turning the bottom one upside down and placing the other one on top—I not only raised the plant above others of the same height, I also gave the whole display a fresh look. The same goes for the large white pot placed on a stool behind the chair (see picture, right). Normally, a large potted plant such as this is placed on the floor, but raising it up changes the entire dynamic of the room. It is small things like this that take your styling to the next level. And yes, pun intended.

LEFT
Pellaea rotundifolia (button fern), left, and *Codiaeum variegatum* (croton) on a table.

BELOW
A large *Philodendron bipinnatifidum* (horsehead philodendron) on a pedestal creates a little canopy over the chair, making this a perfect spot to relax.

HOME GROWN

When I first moved back to Baltimore in 2015 I knew I wanted to live in the city but still have a way to escape the traditional headaches of city life—noise, light, and everyday pollution. Most of all, I wanted to find a place surrounded by greenery. In most cases, you'd have to look beyond the city for this. But I somehow found a perfect mix of the two. Resting alongside the Jones Falls River, my wife and I reside in an old cotton mill, built in 1847, which has recently been converted into loft apartments. Living in a mill provides all the benefits you would expect: high ceilings, original wood floors, stone columns, and, best of all, large windows. The latter are especially important if you're into plants and were probably the main reason we decided to move into this particular apartment. Not to mention the fact that we have a corner unit with four 8 x 4-foot (2.5 x 1.2-m) windows and, below them, the perfect view of a flowing river. Just as a shell, with nothing in it, the apartment had great bones. It just took a few creative touches and a couple of green thumbs to make it home.

When you enter the apartment, you immediately step into our living room. The first thing you're taken by is the height of the ceilings. Here the ceilings are 16 feet (5m) tall, which makes the walls below perfect for use as gallery display areas. The art, like most of the furniture in our home, has a bit of a history, a backstory. That's what separates your place from those belonging to others—the unique pieces that feature there and help tell your story. The details of our homes are what makes and keeps them fresh. When guests come over, they should always have the opportunity to discover something new—no matter how many times they've been before. In our case, whether it's the small knives on the end table or the information in the framed letter written by a friend. Providing scope for discovery in your home will always keep it fresh and new for guests and, more importantly, you.

OPPOSITE

A view of the living room in our Baltimore home. Frank, our fiddle-leaf fig, helps set the tone of the space.

The second element you'll notice about our home is our clear love for greenery. We house over 175 plants throughout. Some have been with us for years, others are the babies of mother plants we own, and some are new to the fold. Our statement plant—Frank, our fiddle-leaf fig—sits in the living room. He sets the tone for the entire apartment. But, as you enter the living room, it's not just Frank and the other plants that overwhelm the space. We've also been able to find a good way to balance the greenery with the art and furniture. In some cases, I've found ways to merge the three. For example, we have a terrarium lamp, which is literally a fillable glass lamp that I decided would make more sense planted as a terrarium rather than filled with stones or seashells. To find out how to create one of these, see *Making a Lamp Terrarium*, pages 62–65. There is also a jungle bar, which consists of an overgrown *Epipremnum aureum* (golden pothos) that droops its vines

around our bar cart. The decision to go with the pothos with the bar cart was based on the fact that this part of the room receives medium to low light and a pothos can survive there. I also think using plants with vines is a good way to tie your plants and furniture together. You can easily manipulate vines to creep along a wall or, in this case, down and through a bar cart. In fact, we are always looking for ways to blur the line between interior and exterior throughout our home.

Continue through our home and you are led past the kitchen and down a hallway that's dressed to impress. Here, to the right, sits another large window and windowsill, which houses over 30 cacti and succulents. We refer to this window as "The Desert." I'm sure you can understand why. The decision only to have small plants there was based on what's happening on the wall across from this window—and that's our propagation station, or what we call

"The Cradle Wall." This is made up of my personally designed propagation vessels, which I call Cradles. Here, there are 16 cradles, which hold 63 cuttings. When Fiona and I first moved into our apartment, we knew we wanted another statement piece. Something that would make our guests stop in their tracks and, for us, would make us want to look at it forever. We tossed around the idea of creating a living wall, but after doing some research we soon figured out that this was out of our budget and not something we'd want to invest in while renting. So, after sleeping on it, I thought about the spice rack I was already using as a vessel for propagation. And it was then that I thought, why not have multiple vessels like this full of cuttings on the wall? This way, we not only have a living propagation wall, but also space to continue growing our plant family. When friends and family come over to visit, they can also pull from the wall to add to theirs.

I thought adding a neon sign would be a nice touch and asked Fiona what she thought it should say. Without hesitation, she suggested the word "house" in green neon. She said, "Get it? It'll be a 'green' house!" She's so cute. For us, having the propagation wall has surpassed our expectations. The cuttings stay rotating in and out, which keeps the wall fresh and forever changing. A consistent work in progress, if you will. Of all the housewarming gifts we gave ourselves, the propagation wall has truly been the gift that keeps on giving.

Lastly, if you make your way to our bedroom, you'll first notice that the ceiling height increases from 16 feet (5m) to 22 feet (7m). This room not only has the most space vertically, but it also receives the most light. There are two large windows that sit in two walls of the room. Given that this room gets the most light, it also gets the most plants. What makes this room stand out is the nook we created in one window and the plant hammock over the bed. Since our windows are so large, and the sills are about 2 feet (60cm) deep, we thought a window seat looking down to the river below was a no-brainer. So, we asked my mother-in-law to make a custom pillow for us to sit on and then we surrounded this with greenery. This is now the perfect spot for weekend coffee hangouts, or where you might find Fiona reading a book.

Across from the window nook you'll find a large *Nephrolepis biserrata* 'Macho' (macho fern) which sits in a plant hammock. Yes, I did say plant hammock. I somehow convinced Fiona to macramé a sort of hammock so I could hang large plants over our heads while we sleep. And can you believe she was actually okay with that? I mean, there was a little resistance in the beginning, but she agreed once I had sketched it out and promised her how cool (and also safe) it would be. I think we made the right decision. If you'd like to make one of these for yourself, see *Making a Plant Hammock*, pages 46–51.

ABOVE

My first lamp terrarium was created because I found this fillable glass lamp base at a store and knew I needed to put something cool inside.

OPPOSITE

This Cradle wall holds 66 cuttings. Most are from our own plants, while others were given by friends and family. While many of the cuttings root and live on the wall, others are potted up, then given as gifts or added to our collection.

MAKING A PLANT HAMMOCK

What happens when your mother offers you an extremely large philodendron, but you don't have any more floor space for it? Well, for me, I decided to look up. Realizing we weren't using the high ceilings in our home effectively, I suggested to Fiona that we hang the philodendron on the wall—not just any wall, but the wall behind our bed so a plant could hang over it like a canopy. Of course, her first concern was that I was losing my mind and her second was that it might fall on us as we slept. Fiona had been creating macramé hangers for a few of our plants and I wondered if she could make a really large one that would work in the same way as a hammock. So, to ease her mind, I sketched out my idea to show her how amazing it could look and assured her that we'd use the proper hardware to secure it to the wall! Somehow this worked, she was on board, and the plant hammock was born. Once we mounted the hammock on the wall and added the philodendron, we couldn't believe how much it surpassed our expectations.

Since then I have rotated different plants in and out of the hammock to see which works best for us. At the end of the day, it's this look that brings the "wow" factor to our bedroom. If you want to make a smaller hammock than the one shown here, just scale down the measurements. Please note: if you follow the instructions carefully and ensure that the wall fixtures you use can support the weight of your potted plant, all should be well, but hanging the hammock above your bed is done at your own risk.

OPPOSITE

This dramatic *Nephrolepis biserrata* 'Macho' (macho fern) in a plant hammock really helps to set the tone and atmosphere of the bedroom in our main home.

1 Measure out a piece of rope, 14 feet (4.3m) long. Align that cut piece with your roll of rope and cut eleven more pieces of the same length. You should now have twelve pieces of rope, each measuring 14 feet (4.3m).

2 On a flat surface, take the ropes and loop them halfway through one of the hitching rings so you now have 24 pieces of rope to work with, each approximately 7 feet (2.1m) long.

3 Attach the ropes to the ring with a gathering knot. To do this, measure and cut a 60-inch (152-cm) piece of rope. Make a 5-inch (13-cm) loop at one end and position this so the open side is facing the ring.

4 Start wrapping the long tail of the 60-inch (152-cm) piece of rope around all the other ropes, including the loop, so they are tightly bound together. You should wrap the ropes at least six or more times. Thread the tail end through the bottom of the loop.

5 Pull the tail that's facing the ring tightly to draw the loop inside the coils. You will end up with two long ends (5a). Cut them for a clean look.

6 Separate the 24 ropes into six sets of four and begin making a square knot with the first set. There will be two working ropes and two "lazy" ropes in each set of four. It is important to keep the ropes in order so your hammock will be flat at the end. You do this in two main stages, working first on Row 1 and then on Row 2.

what you'll need

Measuring tape

180 feet (55m) of 24-lb (11-kg) cotton rope

Sharp scissors

2 heavy-duty hitching rings with wall mounts

8 screws and wall anchors

Your choice of potted plant

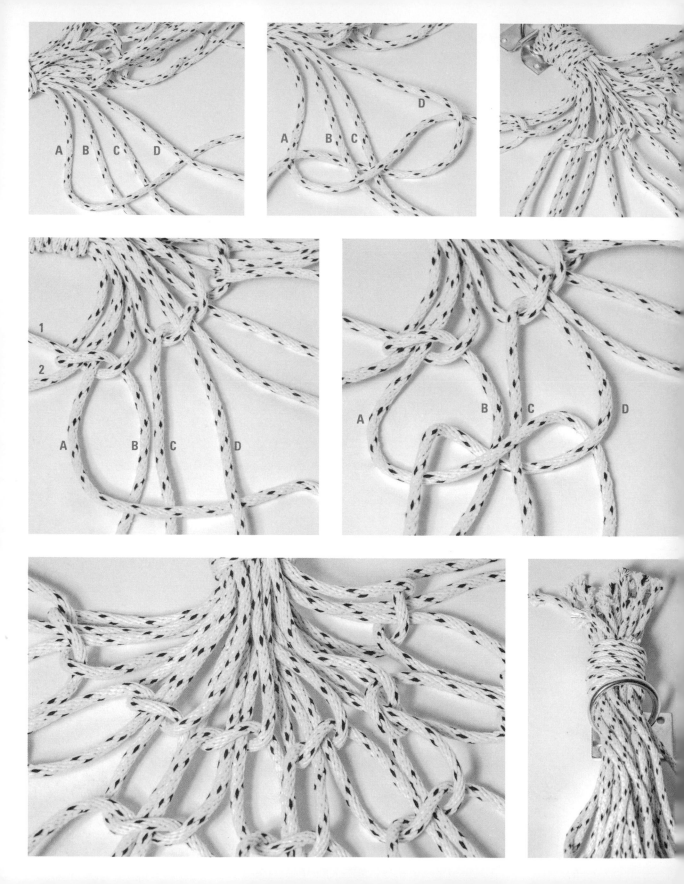

7   For Row 1: On the first set of four ropes, bring rope A in front of B and C, then behind D.

8   Then bring rope D behind C and B, and through the loop made by A, from back to front.

9   Repeat Steps 7 and 8 with the other five sets of rope. You've now completed your first row of square knots.

10 For Row 2: Take the two far ropes on the left (1 and 2) and push them to one side. Take the next four ropes to create a new group of ABCD (formerly CA and DB). Bring rope A in front of B and C, then behind D.

11 Then bring rope D behind C and B, and through the loop made by A, from back to front.

12 Repeat these steps with the other four sets of ropes. You should be left with two single ropes at the end, on the right hand side.

13 To complete the hammock portion, repeat the steps for Row 1 and then Row 2 until you reach the desired length. Make sure the spaces between each row of knots is the same, about 6 inches (15cm). If you want the hammock to have a tighter mesh, you can decrease this distance. Also leave enough of a tail so you can knot it around the other hitching ring.

14 Once you have completed the hammock portion, thread the remaining 24 ends through the second hitching ring and repeat Step 3, making another gathering knot to tie off the hammock.

15 Secure the hitching rings to the wall using the appropriate tools and wall anchors, making sure that what you use can hold the weight of your chosen plant.

16 Hang the hammock carefully on the wall and place a potted plant inside—here I used a *Nephrolepis biserrata* 'Macho' (macho fern).

MAKING A PLANT THRONE

Whenever I'm given the opportunity to style a space in my home or the homes of others that is perfect for curling up with a book and a morning cup of coffee, taking a nap, or just escaping the realities of the world, I don't hesitate to jump right at it. I like to refer to these pockets of green goodness as "plant thrones." And it goes without saying that every castle needs a throne. Throughout this book, I've styled various types of plant thrones, but find they are most suitable for a bedroom or living room. These are typically the places we go to relax, and creating a little space in those rooms to completely submerge yourself in greenery can have a huge impact on the mood and feel of your space, and, most of all, you. Remember to use plants that work best in your home, with the light you have available, and what work best for your care level. So with that said, let's create one for you.

what you'll need

Comfortable chair or chaise longue

Selection of plants of various heights

Pot for each plant in a range of styles and shapes

1   At first glance, a plant throne might seem to be all about the plants, but it really starts with the throne. Choosing the right chair or chaise longue will set the tone for the types of plants with which you surround it. The throne must be eye-catching, but comfort should be the key factor influencing your choice. You want something you wouldn't mind being curled up in for hours. Once you've found comfort, look for style. Make the throne yours by its look. I like chairs with some texture or "grit" so they pop out among the smooth texture of the foliage. It doesn't matter how the rest of the room is styled, take this opportunity to get a little funky with your throne. Remember, this is your space to escape. Once you've selected your throne, you'll need to position it in the perfect spot in your room.

2. Pick a spot next to a window, not only to provide sufficient light for the plants, but also so you have a view to gaze at when you're relaxing. Ideally, I like to create plant-thrones so that they face the entryway of the room—this ensures that whenever you or a guest enter, it's instantly inviting and pulls you in. A clear sign of good design is when you feel compelled to enter a space and never want to leave. This is one of the goals of a plant throne.

3. Surround the throne with plants using the layering method (see page 37). The key word to keep in mind here is "lush." You want the plants to create a slight canopy so you feel fully immersed when sitting on your throne. Start with the larger plants at the back and work your way to the front, scaling down the plants as you do so. I like using tropical plants with large foliage at the back, as they tend to want to spread around the throne, so helping to create that jungle feel—I used *Ficus lyrata* (fiddle-leaf fig), *Livistona chinensis* (Chinese fan palm), and *Phoenix roebelenii* (Pygmy date palm). Try sprinkling in a few plants with different colored foliage or flowers, such as *Stromanthe sanguinea* 'Triostar', *Strelitzia reginae* (bird of paradise), or *Philodendron* 'Rojo Congo' (3a). This splash of color will give depth to the greenery and also be more appealing visually. In the foreground, smaller plants with interesting foliage work best—I used *Zamioculcas zamiifolia* (fern arum/ZZ plant), *Sansevieria trifasciata* (snake plant), and *Monstera deliciosa* (Swiss cheese plant).

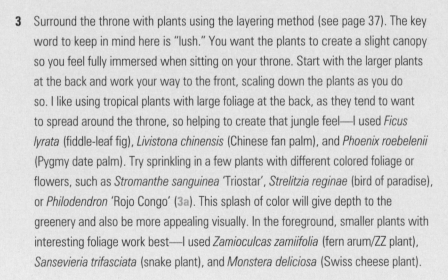

4. Picking the right pots is key. You want pots that fit the look and feel of the throne, so choose those that complement it with their color and shape. Varying the style and shape of the pots here will help frame the throne and add a little extra to the appearance of the plants they hold.

5. Lastly, take a seat. You deserve a break. Remember, this is your throne, in your castle. You can do what you want there.

The living room in my studio is how
I want every room in my life to feel.
A place that just makes you want to kick
off your shoes, take your hair down, and
let the vibes carry you away.

JUNGLE BY THE FALLS

I decided I needed a studio so that I had a space other than my home in which to create, but also one where I could share my passion for green interiors with others. Many people had reached out to me to do photoshoots and events in my home and, knowing Fiona and I weren't particularly fond of opening up our home in this fashion, I thought why not design and create a space with a similar look and feel that creatives could rent out from time to time. What came from that decision is my studio—what I now call Jungle by the Falls. Just like my home, my studio is located in a renovated old mill along the Jones Falls River, hence the name Jungle by the Falls. Just like the mill in which we live, JBTF benefits from the same features: large windows, high ceilings, hardwood floors, and so on. So, again, I'm already starting with a space that has great structure. It will just take the right touches to make it sing.

When you first enter the space, after walking up a flight of stairs, you find the bedroom to the right. I have already explored the health benefits of having plants in the bedroom (see page 17), but what about just because they look amazing? This bedroom has three very large windows. Larger, in fact, than the ones I have in my home. And, as I've said before, where there is light, there is green. I decided to put that statement to the test here. When you enter the bedroom, the first thing that comes to mind is a jungle. This room sets the tone instantly. On one side of the bed stands the room's statement piece: Treezus, another fiddle-leaf fig. Larger than Frank, this fiddle was specifically purchased for the space and has been living his best life, receiving early morning sun and bright indirect light throughout the rest of the day. To his right, I've placed a grouping of cacti and, to the right of that, what many would call the perfect "plant throne." Here you'll find a high-back chair consumed by the large foliage of two *Strelitzia reginae* (bird of paradise), two *Livistona chinensis* (Chinese fan palm), a *Ficus lyrata* (fiddle-leaf fig), a *Philodendron* 'Rojo Congo', a *Monstera deliciosa*

Fiona probably wouldn't agree, but I personally like the studio bedroom better than the one we share at home.

(Swiss cheese plant), and a few odds and ends. (See *Making a Plant Throne*, pages 52–55, if you'd like to find out how to create your own special green corner.)

Given how much bright indirect light the bedroom sees, my options were endless when it came to what plants to bring in. Here is where I do my best job of utilizing the layering technique (see page 37). This corner of the bedroom is flanked by two large windows, so I was able to layer the larger plants to the back, against one window, while letting the smaller plants cascade toward the front. I've also taken advantage of the high ceilings and exposed wooden beams by hanging plants from them. Fiona probably wouldn't agree, but I personally like the studio bedroom better than the one we share at home.

The windows in the studio living room aren't as large the windows in the bedroom, or any of the windows in my main home, so I had to plant accordingly. Given that this room faces northwest, it doesn't see much direct sunlight until late afternoon/early evening. So plants such as *Beaucarnea recurvata* (ponytail palm),

OPPOSITE
A plant throne and gallery wall in the corner of the living room at Jungle by the Falls.

Spathiphyllum wallisii (peace lily), and *Sansevieria trifasciata* (snake plant), as well as other low-light-tolerant plants consume the darker areas of the room, while cacti and philodendrons live in the brighter spots. When I style a place with plants, I like to consider how each plant can bring something new, something more dynamic to the space. So here, instead of having all the greenery in pots at eye level or even in traditional hanging planters near windows, I decided to break up the space by placing a potted *Ravenea rivularis* (majestic palm) on the end of the kitchen bar. This draws your eye upward and accentuates the high ceilings, making the "jungle" feeling more real. I think having this set-up as the first thing you see on entering that part of the studio does so much. Once you pass the palm, you're met with a living room styled in the only way I thought right for the space—the vintage couch, custom-made coffee table, and bookshelves really make the space unique. The addition of green is then the sprinkles and icing on the cake.

Overall, having another living/working space like this gives me the freedom to try out other styling methods. It also gives other people the chance to peek into the spaces I like to create, which hopefully inspires them to create their own. At the end of the day, Jungle by the Falls is our home, a half mile away from home.

ABOVE

A plant display on my coffee table—smaller plants in cool pots are perfect for this. I used *Ficus elastica* (rubber plant) and *Nephrolepis* (lemon button fern).

LEFT

Plants in the bedroom can improve the quality of the air, helping you to get a good night's sleep.

BELOW

Some of my favorite little cacti (including an agave plant, *Cereus repandens* (Peruvian apple cactus), and *Parodia magnifica*) sit together in a group in the living room of my studio.

MAKING A LAMP TERRARIUM

have you ever wondered if we're all just living in one large lamp terrarium ourselves? I sure have. I've always been a fan of miniature or small-scale worlds. As a kid I would find so much joy in creating dioramas out of Popsicle sticks, twigs, and bits of greenery I found around the neighborhood. So, it was only natural when I first began to style my home with plants that I saw the terrarium as a real-life miniature world, which I could design and see thrive for years to come. When I was looking for a lamp for our living room, I knew I wanted something unique—it wasn't until I came across this fillable lamp that the idea of creating a terrarium inside came to me. Yes, the shell of the lamp would be similar to that of anyone else who purchased the lamp, but what was placed inside wouldn't be as cool and creative as what I was going to use. So, I want to help you to create your own terrarium or lamp terrarium at home.

When selecting terrarium plants, ensure they will thrive in the spot you've chosen for the terrarium. Unless your plan is to place a grow light bulb in the lamp, you'll have to depend on the light from a nearby window to keep your plants thriving. Good plant choices include air plants, *Fittonia albivenis* Argyroneura Group (nerve plant), *Ficus pumila* (creeping fig), and ferns such as *Adiantum raddianum* (Delta maidenhair fern) and *Pellaea rotundifolia* (button fern).

| 2 | 3 | 4 | 5 |

what you'll need

Fillable glass lamp or vessel

Small stones

Horticultural charcoal

Terrarium spatula

Potting mix

Small spade or spoon

Your choice of plants

Long scissors

Long tweezers

Piece of terrarium moss mat and other mosses

Couple of large stones and small branches

Miniature figurine

Terrarium glue (optional)

Plant mister

1   If you are using a glass lamp, make sure the wiring comes out of the lid and not the base.

2   Place an inch of small stones at the bottom of the lamp or vessel, making sure to spread them out evenly.

3   Sprinkle an inch of horticultural charcoal on top of the stones. Use the terrarium spatula or your hands to spread the charcoal out evenly.

4   Scoop in the potting mix, making sure that wherever you'll be placing plants, they'll have at least an inch of dirt below them.

5   Start adding the plants. Create little holes in the dirt where you want to position your plants and begin dropping them in. Use the spatula to move the potting mix to one side so you can fit in more plants. Here, I chose a philodendron, a *Davallia canariensis* (hare's foot fern), and a *Pellaea rotundifolia* (button fern) because of where I had decided to position the lamp in my home and the type of light and moisture that these plants require.

6 Cut a piece of terrarium moss mat to the shape you need to cover the surface of the potting mix. Use the tweezers to tuck the mat in gently around your plants.

7 Use the tweezers again to decorate the insides of the lamp with more moss to your liking. The idea is to make the terrarium look and feel like its own little world, so get creative and have fun!

8 I like to add stones and small branches that I find outside. Use the scissors to cut away any dead leaves or ends before positioning these in the terrarium.

9 Using your tweezers, take your figurine— here I used a model of a caribou—and place it in the scene. Stand the figurine upright, either tucking it into a place where it is supported or use some terrarium glue to hold it in position.

10 Lastly, I like to mist the inside of the terrarium with a little water. This water will recirculate through the terrarium, which creates a self-contained ecosystem when you put on the top. Put the top on and place the terrarium in a spot that works for the plants you've chosen. Don't put your terrarium in a spot that gets direct sun. I've had the best luck with terrariums in positions that get bright indirect light.

| 6 | 7 | 8 | 9 | 10 |

caring for your terrarium

If you've purchased plants that require a lot of moisture and the terrarium seems too dry inside, then don't be afraid to take the top off and spray more water inside. The same goes for plants that don't like being constantly wet. If there is too much condensation inside the terrarium, don't hesitate to take the top off and let it air for a while.

NOTE: Make a lamp terrarium at your own risk. All lamps or vessels aren't the same, so making sure the wiring isn't exposed on the inside of the terrarium is key.

living with plants

Plants are a part of my story. I love

mixing and matching different types of

plants throughout my home, sometimes

grouping like plants together and, other

times, blending unlikely pairings

PLANTS IN THE HOME

If you're anything like me, you probably find yourself looking for inspiration in the greenery around you everywhere you go. I find myself walking up to plants in friends' homes, talking to them, inspecting them, and ultimately trying to give my two cents' worth to their owners on how they can help their green friends live better lives. I'm sure some of this falls on deaf ears but, believe me, I get it. I can see how it might be a bit intimidating and stressful to have someone like myself walking around your home looking at your plants—especially if those plants aren't living their best lives. Some friends think I'll be judgmental and reprimand them on their plant care (or lack thereof). But, to be honest, I only want to help and give as much support to their green passion as is called for.

I feel fortunate to know some really talented people who inspire me in so many ways. But it is their decisions on home décor and the ways in which they curate their spaces that spark most excitement in me. In this chapter, I wanted to feature some of the spaces I have had the pleasure to style with plants, and also reveal how I helped guide their owners. My wife and I live in a loft apartment with very large windows that bring in a lot of wonderful light. The ceilings are 20 feet (6m) tall, which allows us to grow large trees. These two factors—the light and the height—enable us to have lots of plants and are the reason why they thrive in our space. Not everyone has a space like ours, however. So, I thought it important to showcase homes that are different to mine and which might resemble yours more closely. Whether you have an old country house or rowhome (terraced house), there are many ways to bring plants into your home. If you provide them with the right conditions and care, you can ensure they thrive and live on. Sometimes you just need to know exactly what types of plants to choose and where to place them. I have provided four Home Tours to show you how this was done in a few of my friends' homes and shared the tips I gave them to help make their living spaces more "jungle-fied."

OPPOSITE

A peek into the bedroom of Jungle by the Falls. As seen here, Treezus, the fiddle-leaf fig, and smaller plants such as a spider plant, a Peruvian apple cactus, and a variegated rubber plant really set the mood of the room.

HOME TOUR:
JAMIE CAMPBELL AND DRURY BYNUM
ASSIGNMENT: TO PLANT-STYLE A
KITCHEN "GREENHOUSE" WINDOW

here aren't many people in my life who have a home that can make me feel as relaxed and at peace as my own, but Jamie and Drury have found a way to do just that with their center-hall Georgian house (built in 1938) in Baltimore. They share this home with their new puppy, Kiwi. It has all the wonderful touches you'd expect in the home of two filmmakers and artists. Before, as you moved through the space, you would initially be taken by all the amazing art these two have collected over the years and curated on the walls and tables, and in corners. By using the interior as if it were a personal art gallery or museum, Jamie and Drury have created a living space that tells a story and leaves a lot to be discovered during future visits.

Now you notice all the plants Jamie has brought into the house, which have begun to compete with the

OPPOSITE
The screened-in porch, where Jamie and Drury enjoy entertaining and spending their downtime, is the perfect spot for their plants in spring and summer. The plants set the mood of the space, which provides them with a relaxing getaway even while they are at home.

BELOW

Tillandsia streptophylla, *Pilea peperomioides* (Chinese money plant), and *Aloe vera* grouped on a dining table make for an eye-catching display.

> "In the warmer months, the outside porch, the plants on the porch, and the sounds of the birds make me feel like I'm somewhere else—a tropical vacation every morning when I have my coffee."

art. As Jamie says, "I've always had plants in my life because my mother had a lot of plants in our house growing up, but in my 20s I found my life plant-less as I wasn't in a place to take care of living things. So, in my 30s and 40s—as I became a more responsible human—I began cultivating that part of my life again." She admits that the process has been slow, but over the past few years she's seen her plant family grow exponentially.

I've personally seen this sort of shift using plants in a lot of my friends' homes, and wondered what inspired Jamie to "jungle-fy" her space. "Moving into this house eight years ago and feeling settled has given me a need for more living things and growing things at home. I've been getting inspiration from a few sources—the incredible homes of my friends (especially you, Hilton!), Pinterest, and home stylists like Justina Blakeney.

Plus, trips to Terrain, a plant nursery in Pennsylvania, have all added up to an incurable plant addiction." I love the fact that she thinks her plant addiction is incurable. I'm sure so many of you can relate to that. "Hi, I'm Hilton Carter, and I am a plant addict." There, I said it.

This addiction has taken hold of so many of us and, honestly, can anyone really blame us? Filling your home with greenery adds so much beauty and vibrancy to life. Some lucky people even have outdoor living spaces that provide an even closer tie to nature (although indoor gardeners can worry less about bugs). Jamie and Drury's porch is just such a space and everything else. As Jamie explains, "In the warmer months, the outside porch, the plants on the porch, and the sounds of the birds make me feel like I'm somewhere else—a tropical vacation every morning when I have my coffee."

It is this appreciation of beauty that turns an avid "green-thumber" into a full-on plant hoarder. However, if not done correctly, it can create a lot of chaos and imbalance. That's where understanding how to style your space comes into play. When I was tasked with the job of plant-styling Jamie and Drury's kitchen "greenhouse" window, I wasn't exactly sure what would work. When we talked about it, Jamie said, "The greenhouse above the sink in my kitchen had always been overlooked. I put only a few plants in there and my cookbooks because I needed to store the books somewhere, and it's a hard-to-reach place, so I didn't want to put too many plants there because I was afraid they might not get enough care if I couldn't get to them with ease."

After realizing this, I knew exactly what needed to be done. Since the window is northwest-facing and full of bright indirect light all day, my options were pretty much endless when it came to the variety

ABOVE
Dressing the top of a coffee table with small succulents and air plants is another way to spread your love of greenery throughout the home. Air plants are flexible friends—they can be placed in a bowl or on a plate and also don't take up too much space.

ABOVE

My main aim when I styled the greenhouse window was to make better use of the space and give it a distinctive look. I used striking plants such as *Gymnocalycium*, *Zamioculcas zamiifolia* (fern arum/ ZZ plant), golden barrel cactus, *Echinocactus*, *Parodia*, and sago palm.

RIGHT

The window before I added my two cents' worth.

of plants that could be grown, but not their size. I was also mindful of the amount of time Jamie could devote to care. With this in mind, I decided Jamie needed a variety of small plants and pots that would fit the space. She also needed low-maintenance plants that did not steal time away from her busy schedule or become neglected over time. And, lastly, the plants had to be unique, so guests would be instantly drawn into the space. Jamie comments, "Hilton saw that as an opportunity to create a cacti garden. Brilliant! The layering of smaller plants in the front and larger cacti at the back created an environment of plants that didn't need a ton of watering and care, but made a huge impact visually. Drury says that it's like a little 'city' of growing things now." So, I guess I created a little version of Arizona for them. That sort of excitement is everything to me! Being able to provide Jamie and Drury with a little help in a big way makes all the difference. The cacti city was a good idea, but the idea didn't just end with purchasing the cacti. The finishing touches were provided by the collection of different pots in which the cacti are planted. This helped to create and complete the look.

When asked how my approach to the greenhouse window has helped her when looking to style other areas of her home, Jamie said, "Adding the smaller plants of different shapes and textures made me realize it's not size that matters, but variation and harmony. I love this greenhouse now, and it's a whole new world that I can admire every time I wash dishes!"

BRENNA MATHERS
AND ELAN KOTZ
ASSIGNMENT: TO PLANT-STYLE THEIR HOME

brenna and Elan live in a newly rehabbed rowhome (terraced house) in the heart of Remington, a small neighborhood in the city of Baltimore, with their dog Moses. Here, you'll often hear the term "charm city" loosely thrown around. However, the true charm comes from homes like theirs and the people that live in them. Many friends have asked me to help them bring plants into their homes, but when Brenna and Elan approached me to plant-style theirs, I instantly saw their genuine enthusiasm for adding more greenery. As Elan says, "We rehabbed this house, and were lucky to gain some really great light and windows. Our old studio was dark and growing plants was a chore, when even possible. Our goal was to really take advantage of the light."

Having the right light is essential and seeing that Elan knew this helped guide my planning for them. When I talked to Brenna, I discovered that she was looking for companionship, too. "When you surround yourself with life and living things, you feel that energy. To me, and aside from our dog, plants are the best company to keep. Bonus: you don't have to entertain them as you would other living things. A little love, maintenance, and H2O yield so many more benefits and much more enjoyment as homeowners. Bringing plants into the new house was a no-brainer." Sounds like Brenna would rather hang out in a room full of plants and her puppy Moses than spend time with you and me. Brenna, I feel you. Believe me.

Brenna and Elan knew they wanted to be surrounded by greenery, but they weren't sure exactly which plants would work in their space and where they could be placed in their home. I loved the passion they demonstrated in wishing to surround themselves with greenery. To me, that's everything, and inspiration for how to add more can be found everywhere nowadays. For Brenna, getting inspired

BELOW LEFT

Brenna and Elan standing in their bedroom with their dog, Moses, with a striking *Ficus lyrata* (fiddle-leaf fig) in the background.

BELOW RIGHT

I thought adding a group of cacti (agave, *Cereus repandens* (Peruvian apple cactus), and *Parodia magnifica*) at the bottom of Brenna and Elan's stairwell would be a nice touch.

OPPOSITE, TOP LEFT

A small group of
cacti along the ledge
above the staircase
gives the space a little
green life.

OPPOSITE, TOP RIGHT
AND BOTTOM RIGHT

A specimen of
Monstera deliciosa
(Swiss cheese plant),
top, sits next to a
Ficus lyrata (fiddle-leaf
fig), bottom, in Brenna
and Elan's bedroom.

was easy. "Talking about plants with my sister is always a bonding moment. We can talk about new growth and care tactics, and check in from afar regarding living things she/we really care about. She talks about her garden with such joy and I like sharing in that, even if mine is potted in our skinny little rowhome. My mom shared that love, so part of me thinks I'm carrying on her nurturing characteristics."

When taking on the job of plant-styling their space, I knew I needed to provide plants that weren't going to be too far out of their care level or too much of a struggle for them to handle. I realized that, with their busy schedules, the most sensible choice would be low-maintenance plants such as *Sansevieria trifasciata* (snake plant), *Zamioculcas zamiifolia* (fern arum/ZZ plant), and a variety of cacti. But I also wanted them to have larger plants to help bring out that "jungle" look and challenge them to become better plant parents. To achieve this, I added a large *Ficus lyrata* (fiddle-leaf fig) and *Ravenea rivularis* (majestic palm), just to make sure the vibes were right. For Elan, "It's really calming. Especially the fig in our bedroom."

Although I wanted to provide them with a few plants to bring life to their space, I also wanted to be sure that nothing would get in the way. So, I tucked a group of cacti on the landing of the staircase and a ZZ plant at the top of the stairs. It also helps that the staircase gets really great light from two windows on the landing. As Elan says, "The most unexpected spot is our stair landing, where there are a lot of cacti and an agave plant. Every time we get to go up and down the stairs, it's an awesome treat." For Brenna, "I've always loved the evening light that comes in on our ledge, but I put all my love and attention into what that looks like and never looked down. The corner below, that Elan mentioned, is for sure perfect for us. It is a statement when you're in the kitchen, dining room, and on the stairs. It brought life to an otherwise dead space with a previously not-so-pretty-view."

Brenna and Elan didn't have much on the landing and staircase, and I was inspired by the great light that pours in there. So much so that the ledge running along the staircase is where I felt the small grouping of cacti would thrive, as well as look amazing—especially the contrast of the terracotta pots against the white-painted brick wall. There's just something so gorgeous in the way the afternoon light shines into that window and caresses the wall, creating really stark shadows.

> "When you surround yourself with life and living things, you feel that energy. To me, and aside from our dog, plants are the best company to keep."

OPPOSITE
A view into the living room. I thought the addition of a *Ravenea rivularis* (majestic palm) would make this room feel more relaxing and inviting.

BELOW
Looking into the bedroom from the hallway. I placed a *Zamioculcas zamiifolia* (fern arum/ZZ plant) outside, as these plants do really well in low light and this part of the home receives medium light.

In the living room, I felt there should only be a few touches of green, given that the windows look out onto a covered porch and that portion of the house doesn't get much bright light. So, I opted for a majestic palm, which only requires medium light, and a small snake plant. I thought placing the palm to the side of an armchair and letting it hang slightly over the side, creating a sort of canopy, would make that corner a bit more desirable. When I asked Elan how it makes him feel, he said, "Our happy place is Casa de Las Olas in Tulum, Mexico. When I look up from my chair and see the palm, I'm reminded of Olas and can't help but feel a sense of peace."

When I considered their bedroom, where they get the most bright indirect light, I knew that this was the spot for a fiddle-leaf fig. They already had a *Monstera deliciosa* (Swiss cheese plant) there, but I knew the fig would bring a little more character to the room. Their home has a real minimalistic charm, with everything in its place, so I didn't want to just toss in any plant randomly and overwhelm the space, especially where they rest their heads. Given that the fiddle-leaf fig has a beautiful, tree-like shape, I knew it wouldn't take up too much floor space and that the growth would happen up above. Luckily, there are high ceilings in their bedroom, so a thriving fiddle has plenty of room to stretch its arms there.

Overall, when styling someone's home with plants, I think you first need to establish their level of knowledge of the care required for the plants you might use. Once you're aware of this, you can set them up for success. Knowing Brenna and Elan the way I do, I believe they'll be just fine.

HOME TOUR:
JESSICA AND MICHAEL KREMEN
ASSIGNMENT: TO DESIGN AND STYLE THE FAMILY ROOM

Out in the county of Baltimore, surrounded by greenery, sits the lovely home of Jessica and Michael Kremen, their kids, Lily and Gus, and their pup, Simon. I was really excited when Jessica reached out to me, asking if I'd style her family room, not only because it would be the first family room I'd styled, but also because it was a blank canvas. They had a couch in the family room and that was it. The room was obviously where they and their children spent most of their bonding time. Understanding this and also the ages of the kids—and making sure that things weren't too fragile or in the way—was at the forefront of my mind.

ABOVE
I designed an arched cutout in the gallery wall for Jessica and Michael, so they had a spot that added depth and which could also hold a vase with a leaf cutting.

RIGHT
The Kremen family hanging out in their family room.

ABOVE

I made this lamp terrarium with the kids in mind. The world of a terrarium is so whimsical—it's the perfect piece for a kid.

Jessica trusted my vision when it came to styling the space, but more than anything she really wanted me to add a green touch. She had found inspiration for bringing greenery into her home after visiting my studio space, Jungle by the Falls (see pages 56–61). As Jessica recalls, "I didn't know what I was missing until we did a photoshoot at Jungle by the Falls that this was exactly the style I wanted for a room in my home. It was natural and gorgeous, and also do-able for

me." I know it wasn't long after her visit that she reached out and asked me to create the same feeling in her family room. Jessica only had one plant when I first visited and I knew the challenge for me was to provide her with more plants that she would feel comfortable with and also able to care for confidently. I didn't want to just throw any variety her way, which she'd only be able to keep alive for a day or a week, but plants that she and her family could grow with,

hopefully for years to come. The key was finding the right plants that would work in the light they'd get from the windows in the family room.

In Baltimore County, where Jessica and Michael live, you find more outdoor greenery than you do in the city. Large trees surround their home, which can make the family room a bit dark in spring and summer when their full limbs are covered with leaves. But the large windows that make up one of the four walls in the room provide enough medium light for a variety of plants to thrive. I wanted to make the walls in this room fun too, not just for the kids, but also for Jessica and Michael. Knowing the adjacent wall is quite a long way from the windows, I knew I needed to choose plants that would be happy with the low light levels as well as low-maintenance for that area. To the side of the couch, I placed a *Sansevieria trifasciata* (snake plant) and *Zamioculcas zamiifolia* (fern arum/ ZZ plant), which were both just the right size to allow

OPPOSITE, TOP LEFT

Hanging planters holding a pothos
and a heart-leaf philodendron were
added in front of the sliding doors
to make the room feel more lush.

OPPOSITE, BOTTOM LEFT

A single propagation cradle with
a golden pothos cutting hangs
in the middle of the gallery wall,
providing a little loving greenery
among the collection of pictures.

OPPOSITE RIGHT

A dramatic grouping of *Ravenea
rivularis* (majestic palm) along the
sliding doors of the family room.

more light to make its way deeper into the room.
Above these, I hung an *Epipremnum aureum* (golden
pothos), while on the gallery wall I hung two single
propagation Cradles to hold cuttings from the ZZ plant
and golden pothos. This gave the gallery wall a little
green life, but also helped to add a feeling of depth.
Adding depth to a gallery wall is a great way to take
it to the next level. A mixture of flat artwork and
sculptural works is key.

I decided to place most of the plants next to the
windows. This room gets early morning sun, but is
limited to medium light throughout the rest of the day,
so plants such as *Spathiphyllum wallisii* (peace lily),
Monstera deliciosa (Swiss cheese plant), hanging
Epipremnum (pothos), and *Ravenea rivularis* (majestic
palm) felt right for the spot. I knew that providing
little details such as a lamp terrarium, like the one
I have in my own home (see page 44), would be
something the children would really love. So I made
a lamp terrarium especially for them. Terrariums are
like little worlds in themselves, providing kids with a
space to wander through and explore in their minds.

When plant-styling a space, it's easy to just bring
in a few random plants, but the key to introducing
greenery well is to make sure that the plants have the
right pots. Finding the right pots to fit the space, as
well as the color palette you're working with, makes a
world of a difference (see page 34). Given that the pot
can be double the price of the plant, try to find a mix
of planters that are either store-bought, thrift-store
purchases, or repurposed. Once we'd found the right
mix of pots and plants, I knew my job was done and
the family room was complete.

When I asked Jessica how she felt about her newly
plant-styled family room, she said, "I love the room!
I find myself sitting in it alone after I put the kids to
bed, just looking around. It's a room we all spend a lot
of time in and love to be in. My kids love playing with
the pillows on the ground and they love looking at the
gallery wall. They love to help water and inspect the
plants. The plants bring in an adult feel without things
being too fragile. Besides all the health benefits they
add to the space, the natural feel and look the plants
bring can't be replicated." I couldn't agree more!

"I love the room! I find myself sitting in it alone
after I put the kids to bed, just looking around."

OPPOSITE, TOP LEFT
Michelle hanging out
on her screened-in
porch oasis.

OPPOSITE, BOTTOM
LEFT
This cozy corner of
Michelle's living room
is enhanced by a
Monstera deliciosa
(Swiss cheese plant).

OPPOSITE, RIGHT
Using little stools
and tables as plinths,
so the plants sit at
different levels, makes
the arrangement look
more interesting.

HOME TOUR:
MICHELLE GECZY
ASSIGNMENT: TO PROVIDE TIPS ON MAXIMIZING FLOOR SPACE

In this late-1800s home, located in the Roland Park neighborhood of Baltimore City, my friend Michelle Geczy has beautifully crafted a space full of art, texture, and life. I recall entering her home for the first time and initially being taken aback by the welcoming feeling of her living room. Everything is meticulously curated, and placed just where she wishes, while never making the space seem so delicate that guests feel they can't explore. There are books stacked both on and under the coffee table, a mixture of artwork aligning the walls, and small treasures on every surface around the room. While Michelle's style is a bit bohemian, once you look beyond all the amazing furnishings, there is a seamless flow of greenery that weaves its way throughout her home. As Michelle says, "Plants are a part of my story. I love mixing and matching different types of plants throughout my home, sometimes grouping like plants together and, other times, blending unlikely pairings."

> "Plants are a part of my story. I love mixing and matching different types of plants throughout my home, sometimes grouping like plants together and, other times, blending unlikely pairings."

Although there are a lot of green touches throughout Michelle's living space, it was her covered porch that really grabbed my attention. During the warmer months the porch becomes a sort of private nursery or, should I say, personal greenhouse. All Michelle's plant friends, such as her fiddle-leaf figs and cacti and small succulents, get to lounge about as if taking a vacation themselves. "During the summer months I take a lot of plants from inside the house outside onto the screened-in porch or backyard. The palms, succulents, and cacti especially love

OPPOSITE

Michelle's screened-in porch
is the perfect place to move
the plants during the warmer
months of the year.

BELOW

A view into the living room,
showing Michelle's collection
of books, artworks, and other
decorative objects.

the fresh air and sun. It's quite a process to do the mass move of plants indoors
to out or vice versa."

Michelle weaves plants through her home in a way that doesn't feel cluttered or
forced in any way, but at the same time she doesn't shy away from the fact that
they're there. You definitely notice the plants. When talking about what inspired
her, she said, "I grew up on a farm with grass between my toes and wide open
spaces to roam. We didn't spend much time indoors. My parents wanted to raise
my sisters and me in the country, and I developed an appreciation for all things
green from an early age. The joy of being outdoors is a feeling I carry with me, and
I love the juxtaposition of living in the city and creating inspiring green spaces in
and around my home."

This affinity with nature becomes very apparent as you move through Michelle's
home. Her passion for greenery as a child on a farm has bloomed and taken shape
as an adult living in the city. But what I love about her home and the surrounding
neighborhood is that, at times, you can quickly forget you're in a city and be
swept away by the lush local environment. This can be easily glimpsed from her
kitchen windows. When I asked Michelle to name her favorite room, she didn't
hesitate to say the kitchen. "The kitchen perfectly brings the outside inside, and
inside out, year round. The room is mostly windows that face the backyard. During

BELOW

Plants in the bedroom can really set the mood and make the whole space feel more relaxed.

OPPOSITE

A peek into Michelle's kitchen where her breakfast nook has a perfect balance of plants and pillows.

temperate months, I leave the windows open to let in the fresh air and breeze. Built-in wooden benches, just below the windows, provide a welcome space for morning coffee and make for a cozy reading nook."

When Michelle asked me for advice on how to style her plants, there wasn't much I could see that was wrong. Instead, I used my expertise to ensure the plants were not too close to air-conditioning or heat vents. I also explained to Michelle how she could arrange the plants to create a better and more even flow around her dining room. I had noticed, when trying to walk over to a window in the dining room, that there were a few cacti and a palm sitting above

an air-conditioning vent and next to a radiator. They were lined up, but spaced in a way that rather crowded the floor space, making it a little difficult to maneuver around the dining table. I explained to Michelle how layering the cacti would give each of them a moment to shine while also clearing some space in the room. Michelle was pleased with the result, saying: "I have two large windows in the cacti corner in my dining room, which is near a steam radiator and air-conditioning return. A lot of different variables in a contained space by the room's windows. I had the plants more spread out; I like how you grouped them together, away from the heating/cooling variables. I regained access to the main window and also reclaimed floor space. It was a subtle change that made a welcome esthetic and had practical impact. It's helped me think about styling, or restyling, other spaces."

My advice when styling plants in your home is always to think about layering them, so that light can reach every single plant and you're able to reach each one for watering. So, for that particular corner of Michelle's dining room, it made much more sense to place the larger cacti at the back and the small cacti at the front—as you move from the window to the cactus at the very front, there's a nice gradation in size. Think about approaching this design idea in the same way you would set up a family photo. As I'm sure anyone who is tall knows, in situations such as these you're going to the back so that the small folks can be seen at the front. For me, being 6 foot 5 inches tall, I know a lot about playing the background.

chapter four

plant-care essentials

All living things, including us, need some self-care. A little trim here and a little trim there. Your green buds are no different

POTTING YOUR PLANT

bringing your plant home

bringing a new plant home should be such a great feeling. You've just added another member to your plant family and ultimately a little more time to your plant-care schedule. Whether the latter is a good or bad thing for you— hopefully good—you're definitely up for the challenge. You have the spot in your home already selected, your tools are ready, and the new plant is ready to make a seamless transition from the nursery to your home. But I suggest you take a moment before rushing in and pulling the plant out of its nursery pot right away. Instead, I recommend sitting your plant, still in its nursery pot, in the new pot with the base tray underneath, and leaving it for a month in the spot you've chosen for your plant to live in eventually. This will allow the plant to acclimatize to its new surroundings, the light it will receive, and the new watering routine.

During this period of acclimatization, don't be surprised if your plant loses a few leaves. Remember, when you found the plant it was living in a nursery that provided a lot more light than the spot in your home unless, of course, you live in a greenhouse. And if that's the case, when can I move in? This initial loss of leaves is the plant's way of letting you know that it's going to shed what it can no longer support due to its new environment. Once the plant settles in, you should see less leaf loss and some new growth. When I was new to bringing plants into my home, this was the period that freaked me out the most. I would get a plant home, place it in a spot, and then panic when I started to see it dropping leaves. Thinking it was because it needed more light, I'd move it to a new part of the house, unknowingly only adding to the problem. Then, again, that plant tried to acclimatize to its new spot and, of course, lost more leaves. It was a vicious cycle. Learning from my past mistakes really helped me become a better plant parent and, hopefully, this will help you become one as well.

planting in a pot with a drainage hole

Once your plant has acclimatized, you can repot it in the new planter. The best time to repot your plant is on the same day that you plan to water it. Make sure to pot up the plant first before watering, so the potting mix is dry and the plant is easier to transfer from the nursery pot to the new pot. Now you're prepared, here are some tips for repotting your plant.

what you'll need

Gardening gloves

New pot or planter

Small spade or digger (I use an old ice-cream spoon)

Fresh potting mix

Watering can

1 Gently squeeze the sides of the nursery pot with your hands to loosen the potting mix.

2 Grab the base of the plant's trunk or branches, and carefully lift the plant out of the nursery pot.

3 Hold the plant over the new pot. Before placing the plant in the pot, use one hand to gently loosen the roots and potting mix. This separates the roots so that they are no longer bound together.

4 Use the spade or digger to add a few scoops of potting mix to the new pot. Spread the potting mix out evenly over the bottom of the pot—it needs to be at least 2–3 inches (5–7.5cm) deep. Depending on the size of the pot, the ratio of potting mix to pot should be about 1 to 3.

5 Place the plant in its new pot. Add more potting mix all around the plant until it is about 1–2 inches (2.5–5cm) from the top of the pot. Again, this depends on the size of the new pot. I don't like to fill my pots with potting mix all the way to the top, as I like to be able to add more in the future once the roots start growing to give plants an extra nutrient boost (this is known as top-dressing).

6 Gradually pour water around the inside edge of the pot and let the water seep slowly into the potting mix—to ensure it reaches all the roots. Once you see water trickling into the base tray, that's a sure sign that you have given your plant enough water. If your base tray fills up with water, then wait about 15–30 minutes before lifting the pot from the tray and discarding the excess water.

THE DIRT

Using the right potting mix for each type of plant is important, not only for the health and growth of your plants, but also for your stress levels. Potting a plant in the wrong potting mix can lead to its eventual demise and leave you unsure as to the reasons why. While most plants are happy with standard all-purpose potting mix that dries out slowly and retains moisture, cacti and succulents, for example, need a mix that is fast-drying and doesn't contain additional fertilizers. When you're at your local nursery or garden center make sure to ask an assistant which potting mix will work best for each type of plant you buy.

what you'll need

Ruler

New pot or planter

Gardening gloves

Small stones

Horticultural charcoal

Measuring cup or pitcher (jug)

Small spade or digger (I use an old ice-cream spoon)

Fresh potting mix

Watering can

planting in a pot without a drainage hole

I hate to say this, but it seems all the really cool pots and planters these days come without drainage holes. For me, that's a big issue as I don't like potting my plants in pots that don't let me know exactly how much water I'm giving them, or allow me to poke my finger inside the bottom to see where the roots are (in case it's time to repot).

Planting in a pot without a drainage hole is like driving a car blindfold. And you'd never do that, right? I guess it depends on how amazing the pot is, I suppose. So, if that's the way you're thinking, at least let me show you how to pot plants in them correctly; that way, you'll have more confidence when it comes to watering them. My advice is to create a buffer between the bottom of the pot and the potting mix and plant roots. Without that buffer the water has nowhere to go when you water the plant apart from the bottom of the pot—and water sitting at the base of the pot among the plant's roots can eventually lead to root rot. The buffer is created using stones and horticultural charcoal, and gives the water a place to settle and dry up, while the roots and potting mix sit above it.

1   Measure the diameter of the pot. In this example, let's say the pot is 5 inches (13cm) in diameter. You need to fill the pot with small stones to a depth equal to one-tenth of the diameter of the pot. So, for a 5-inch (13-cm) pot, the stones should fill ½ inch (1.25cm) of the pot. Once you've worked out the depth needed for your particular pot, scoop the stones into the bottom and use the ruler to check.

2   Add the same depth of horticultural charcoal. So, in this case, you'd add ½ inch (1.25cm) of charcoal on top of the stones at the bottom of the pot.

3   Fill the measuring cup or pitcher (jug) with water and take a note of how much water it contains. So, in this case, let's say it holds 2 cups (500ml) of water. Start pouring water into the new pot until it reaches the surface of the charcoal. Then pause and note how much water you poured in. If, for example, you poured ½ cup (125ml) of water into the pot, then that is the amount of water you need to give your plant each time you water it. That way, you'll know you are not overwatering and that once the water makes its way through the potting mix and roots, it'll settle in the stones and charcoal. Just make a note—on the pot itself or in a notepad—of the exact amount of water needed for that particular plant and pot.

4   Pour the water from the pot and then use the spade or digger to scoop fresh potting mix on top of the charcoal. You can, if you wish, just use gloved hands to do this.

5   Here, I used a pair of tongs to plant a small cactus in my pot. To finish planting the pot, follow the steps for *Planting in a Pot with a Drainage Hole* (see pages 98–101).

LET THE LIGHT IN

most people understand that plants need water and light to survive. However, not many people are sure—or even aware of—what type of light they have in their homes and what is necessary for their particular plants to thrive. Understanding the different types of light is crucial. Knowing what direction all the windows in your home face will help you to work out the types of light you have coming through those windows.

window direction and light levels

Understanding the types of light you have in your home will make a big difference to the choice of plants you can place in those areas. Here's a breakdown of the types of light your plants will receive in the northern hemisphere, depending on the direction in which a window is facing (these directions will be reversed if you live in the southern hemisphere):

- **NORTHERN EXPOSURE** Medium to bright indirect light
- **NORTHEAST EXPOSURE** Medium to bright indirect light. Depending on the time of year, direct sunlight in the morning
- **NORTHWEST EXPOSURE** Bright indirect light
- **EASTERN EXPOSURE** Direct morning sunlight to bright indirect light
- **SOUTHERN EXPOSURE** Bright indirect light to medium light
- **SOUTHEAST EXPOSURE** Bright indirect light
- **SOUTHWEST EXPOSURE** Bright indirect light to direct afternoon sunlight
- **WESTERN EXPOSURE** Bright indirect light to direct afternoon sunlight

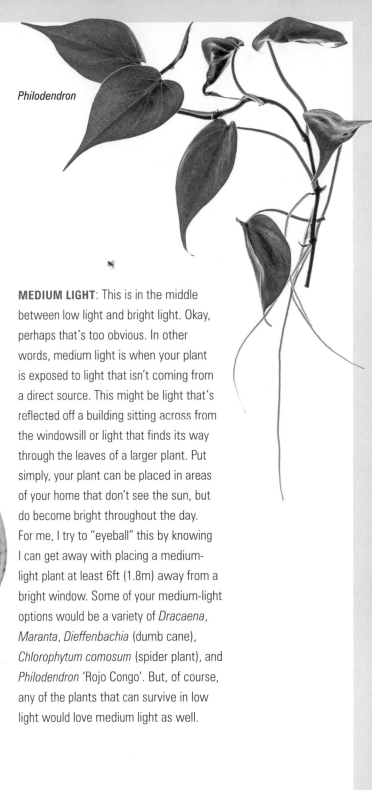

Philodendron

different light categories

For growing greenery indoors, there are four light categories: low light, medium light, bright indirect light, and, lastly, direct sunlight.

LOW LIGHT: This is the least amount of natural light you can give a plant before it will be unable to thrive or produce as much new growth as you'd like. Low light can be gauged either by eye or with a light meter. I often find myself only placing plants in low-light areas because I have a spot in a room that is just calling out for a plant to freshen it up. When this is the case, I use plants that will work in a low-light setting. Your low-light plants include *Epipremnum aureum* (golden pothos), *Calathea lancifolia* (rattlesnake plant), *Zamioculcas zamiifolia* (fern arum/ZZ plant), *Sansevieria trifasciata* (snake plant), and *Spathiphyllum wallisii* (peace lily).

MEDIUM LIGHT: This is in the middle between low light and bright light. Okay, perhaps that's too obvious. In other words, medium light is when your plant is exposed to light that isn't coming from a direct source. This might be light that's reflected off a building sitting across from the windowsill or light that finds its way through the leaves of a larger plant. Put simply, your plant can be placed in areas of your home that don't see the sun, but do become bright throughout the day. For me, I try to "eyeball" this by knowing I can get away with placing a medium-light plant at least 6ft (1.8m) away from a bright window. Some of your medium-light options would be a variety of *Dracaena*, *Maranta*, *Dieffenbachia* (dumb cane), *Chlorophytum comosum* (spider plant), and *Philodendron* 'Rojo Congo'. But, of course, any of the plants that can survive in low light would love medium light as well.

Sansevieria trifasciata

Ficus lyrata

Ficus elastica

BRIGHT INDIRECT LIGHT: Whenever someone asks what type of light their plant will thrive in, I tell them bright indirect light without hesitation. Bright indirect light is everything to every plant. Honestly, I don't believe there is one plant that won't thrive and give you the look you desire when exposed to bright indirect light. But what exactly is it? To me, bright indirect light is when a plant is sitting in a window with full exposure to the outside, while never being exposed to direct sun. This could be because the window doesn't receive much sun or is covered in sheer drapes (curtains). Bright indirect light is basically a filtered and diffused light. Imagine being outside on a cloudy day—the light you experience there is bright indirect light. Your bright indirect light options include *Ficus lyrata* (fiddle-leaf fig), *Ficus elastica* (rubber plant), *Crassula ovata* (money tree), and, honestly, any other type of plant you can find.

DIRECT SUNLIGHT: This is exactly what you think it is. The sun is coming directly into your window and touching your plant. While most of us regard this as harsh and hot exposure, it really depends on the time of day. I always recommend placing a fiddle-leaf fig, for example, in a spot that receives bright indirect light and no direct afternoon sun. That's because morning sun is less harsh and won't burn the leaves of your plants. However, there are some plants, such as desert plants, that love being kissed by the hot sun all day—especially cacti, succulents, and palms.

rotating plants

Make sure to rotate your plants every two months or so. When I first got Frank, my fiddle-leaf fig, I noticed at some point that the branches closest to the window would grow new leaves most consistently. To encourage a balance of growth, rotation is key. So, do it!

CLEANING PLANT LEAVES

Clean the leaves of your plants every three to six months using a little dish soap (washing-up liquid) and water. Keeping leaves free of dust and grime helps to give them their natural shine and allows more light to reach the surface.

LEFT AND BELOW
In the picture below, the leaf on the left had been collecting dust for months, while the one on the right has just been cleaned. The difference is clear—the shine and vibrancy of a clean leaf is everything.

WATERING

ike all living things, plants need water to survive, whether this is drawn up via the roots or pulled as moisture from the air. Although most people know that plants need water, some are unsure how much each of their plants requires. Some have learned to pour tap water into watering cans and let it rest overnight to de-chlorinate and come to room temperature. Others say that it is best to use distilled water. I say that your approach should depend on where you live and the type of water coming out of your faucet (tap). If you're concerned about impurities in your faucet water, then by all means try these methods. But, for me, tap water, straight from the faucet has never been an issue. What I do agree with across the board is making sure the water is lukewarm. No one likes jumping into a freezing cold pool or a hot shower. We all like to be eased into that change, and so do the roots of your plants.

establishing a watering routine

I've found it helpful to have a routine for watering plants. This is where knowing exactly what plants you have and what their care requirements are comes into play. Knowing when your plants need water is then made easy because you simply check the potting mix and water accordingly. Most houseplants, such as *Ficus elastica* (rubber plant), *Strelitzia reginae* (bird of paradise), and any variety of *Philodendron*, like to be watered when the potting mix is dry. In contrast, most ferns prefer their potting mix to remain slightly damp. Knowing this, you can establish a watering routine that is easy to remember and less stressful.

So, let's say your rubber plant is watered on a Saturday and it takes another seven days for the potting mix to dry out. From this you can assume that your rubber plant needs watering every seven days, along with other plants that have dried out over the past week. This seven-day routine is working perfectly until one week you notice that some of the leaves on the rubber plant are starting to turn yellow. You think to yourself, "What's going on here? I've been watering it every seven days like clockwork." The answer is that you haven't been paying attention to the fact that the potting mix hasn't been drying out as fast as it did in the summer. Now it's winter, the potting mix is taking 10 days to dry out. This has thrown out your watering routine, but, because you've been paying attention to the potting mix, you can simply adjust the routine based on the time of year. Subtle adjustments in watering are also required for plants in different parts of your home. Let's take another example: *Sansevieria trifasciata* (snake plant). This plant can thrive in bright direct sun, but also in low-light situations. But you're obviously going to have to water a snake plant in a window that receives full sun more often than a snake plant in a low-light corner of a room—although it's the same type of plant, it has different needs based on where it is positioned. If you can remember that, you'll always water your plants when they need it.

Some of my favorite plants are those that show signs that they need water just by moving their leaves in a certain way. The leaves of *Spathiphyllum wallisii* (peace lily), for instance, will droop when it needs water, while those of *Stromanthe sanguinea* 'Triostar' curl up if it's thirsty. How amazing would it be if all plants told you exactly when they needed something?! Yeah, I know. Amazing. But that's not the world we live in. Most plants need you to notice when they need a drink and, if you're on top of this, then they will thrive.

watering tips and techniques

Here are some general rules of thumb (a green thumb, obviously) for watering houseplants:

1   **GIVE THE RIGHT AMOUNT** My method for judging the right amount of water to give most plants is based on how dry the potting mix is. Most plants like to be watered when the top layer of potting mix is dry. You can gauge this by doing what I call "the finger test." Take your index finger and stick it an inch or two into the potting mix. Don't be afraid to get a little dirty (**1a**). If your finger comes out dry and the dirt falls away easily, your plant is ready to be watered. If your finger is a bit muddy and there is dirt stuck to it, then the potting mix is still sufficiently wet and the plant doesn't need watering. Some plants such as ferns need to be a bit more damp than other plants, so need more water throughout the week, while desert plants like cacti and snake plants prefer to be dry and will only require a drink every few weeks.

2   **WHERE TO WATER** As soon as you know a plant is ready to be watered, you need to figure out the best place to do this. Some of my plants, especially my hanging plants, have to be taken to the kitchen sink or shower to be watered properly and then need time to drain. However, if you have potted plants with base trays, it is easier to water them where they are. I like to water some of my smaller plants thoroughly and so prefer to take them to the sink. This eliminates watering to the point where water is flowing from the base tray onto the floor.

3   **HOW TO WATER** Once you've decided where you're going to water, fill a watering can with lukewarm water. Just as if you were testing the temperature of a baby's bottle, you need to ensure the water you are going to pour over the plant's roots is as close to lukewarm as possible. This may take some time, but it's important to get the water temperature right. Then, slowly pour the water over the potting mix, making sure to get the whole surface area wet. You'll know you've given your plant enough water when you see water seeping into the base tray (**3a**). Taking the time to allow the water to make its way slowly through the potting mix and caress the roots has always made sense to me, given that the faster you pour the water, the faster it will come out the drainage hole. You want to give the roots and potting mix time to hold on to the water as it drains through the pot. This helps the roots grow stronger and makes your plant healthier. For advice on watering a pot without a drainage hole, see Step 3 on page 105.

4 5

4 LET THE PLANT DRAIN Stop watering once you see water filling the base tray, to avoid it overflowing. Let the water sit in the tray for about 15–30 minutes to allow the potting mix and roots to pull back any water they weren't quick enough to grab on its way down. After that time, discard the excess water in the tray. If the plant is small and the pot isn't too heavy, simply lift the pot and place it to one side while you dump the water in the sink. If the plant and pot are heavy, and impossible to lift, wrap the base tray in a towel and let it absorb all the water, or take a baster and suck up the water that way. Honestly, just use whichever method is easiest and least messy for you. The important thing here is to make sure the plant's roots aren't sitting in water.

5 WHAT TO USE I like to use a watering can with a long spout so that I can get to hard-to-reach places, although this isn't necessary. For example, if you're taking your plants over to a shower for watering, then it's easier to run the faucet to water them. If you're outside, just use a garden hose. However, having a watering can that you can use to reach up high to water hanging plants, or to get behind another plant on the windowsill, or which will give you a slower pour, is useful. There are many types of watering cans (see page 25), but I like to use something a bit more stylish, as I know I will be using it at least once or twice a week. I like to place my watering can around the house as if it's just another piece of art. I mean, why not?

GETTING A PLANT SITTER

When you go on vacation, you'll need to find someone to look after your plants—you need a plant sitter! To ensure your plants get the care they need, ideally choose someone who has plants of their own. Make the task easier by placing "same needs" plants together. For instance, group all your cacti in one window or your low-light plants in a corner. This will help the plant sitter identify which plants need what type of care—one group may need watering every three days and another every seven days, for example. Make a color-coded spreadsheet so the plant sitter knows what care to give each group. You can make things even easier for them by using colored notes to label the different groups—perhaps a green note on a fiddle-leaf fig and rubber plant to show they need watering every seven days; a blue note on pots of ferns to indicate they need watering every three days; and a red note on pots of cacti to tell them not to water these at all (because cacti need watering fortnightly and your trip is only 10 days long), and so on. Just make sure it is clear which color goes with which care group on the spreadsheet. Also invite your plant sitter over so you can explain the spreadsheet and demonstrate your watering routine. Lastly, before you leave, set the house temperature to ensure your plants are comfortable. Most indoor plants thrive in temperatures ranging from 65–75°F (18–24°C).

FEEDING

When I was a kid, one of my favorite films was *Little Shop of Horrors*. There was something so interesting about the care the store clerk, Seymour, gave his plant from outer space, even going as far as feeding it his own blood. I'm not suggesting you do this for your plants, but they will need food to stay nourished and grow stronger, just like all living things. I think many people miss this step or just aren't aware of its importance. Put simply, feeding is key if you want a healthy plant. Done only in spring and summer when plants want to grow the most, feeding with an appropriate fertilizer supplies all the nutrients the potting mix has lost over the fall (autumn) and winter as a result of watering. Depending on the type of fertilizer you use, feedings can be as often as every other watering or only every two to three months.

I am often asked whether plants need to be fed immediately on being purchased from a nursery. The answer is that, depending on the time of year you buy the plant, the nursery would more than likely have been feeding it. However, if you're unsure, it's best to ask someone there. So, when you get home, the potting mix should already contain all the nutrients your plant will need to carry it through to the next growing season. After that you'll want to start providing your plant with food.

under- and overfeeding

Signs that you might need to start feeding a plant include poor growth during the spring and summer, when most plants do all their growing, and a lack of bright color in the foliage. Warning signs that you might be overfeeding a plant is when you notice a browning of the leaves soon after a feeding. Make sure to follow the instructions supplied with the fertilizer you're using correctly, so you give your plant the love and attention it needs to thrive and bloom.

SIC TRANSIT GLORIA

All living things, including us, need some self-care. A little trim here and a little trim there. Your green buds are no different. With plants, you sometimes have to cut away the dead to expose a bit of the new. Having browning leaves is just a part of the life cycle of plants, so if you see a yellowing or browning leaf from time to time, it's not always a sign that your plant is in bad shape. When dead leaves appear, manicuring them is important if you want to keep your plant looking its best and also in optimum health. Dying leaves can still pull some of the nutrients necessary for the plant, so it's better to cut them off rather than just letting them die fully attached.

While pruning to remove dead leaves is something you can do throughout the year, pruning back to improve the shape of a plant or to encourage new growth is something I suggest you only do during a plant's growing period. During the colder months, most of your plants will go dormant and new growth will be sparse. So, pruning back healthy parts of your plant is best done during the "growing season."

Pruning is also necessary to guide the plant into taking the shape you want. If your plant starts to extend its limbs too close to a ceiling or into areas of your home where they become unmanageable, then pruning back can help control this. Pruning can also be used to stimulate new growth or encourage a specimen to branch out. Many people ask me how they can get their one-branch *Ficus lyrata* (fiddle-leaf fig) or *Ficus elastica* (rubber plant) to branch out like Frank, and the answer to this lies in pruning. Where the cut is made is essentially where the new growth will form. In settings with good light, most plants will form two new shoots from this cut. When you cut off healthy shoots, the plant thinks it is being harmed and fights back by growing more, as if to say, "I know you're trying to kill me, but I won't allow it." I find that quite amazing.

I also think it's important to prune plants to keep them looking nice and in perfect health, giving them the same level of care as you do yourself. You don't just wake up in the morning and walk out the door, do you? You present yourself in the best possible way— you brush your teeth, wash your face, comb your hair, and so on. I think the same sort of care is necessary for plants. I believe that plants have feelings, so please help them to look their best. They'll thank you for it by continuing to thrive and grow strong.

PROPAGATION

a fresh start

Tradescantia pallida

I became completely enamored with caring for plants for a few reasons, but the one that has had the most lasting impact on me has by far been learning to propagate. Plant propagation basically involves producing a new plant from a mother plant. You hear so much about plant "parenthood," but knowing how to propagate and then watching as your little plant takes shape and develops into a full-grown plant is the very definition of this.

Back in 2014, when I was still quite a novice (aka a brown-thumber), a friend's mother noticed a change in my home—it had gone from being filled with furniture and art and quickly become a living indoor jungle. Seeing my passion developing in front of her eyes, she suggested I start propagating plants in order to accumulate more. Given the cost of plants, I saw this as the perfect way of both saving money and learning a little more about the plants I had, as well as about plant life in general.

So, she quickly showed me the basic steps involved in propagation—you take a cutting from the mother plant and then place it in water. I'm sure she said much more than that, but I took away the idea that you just make a cut from any plant and place the cutting in water. However, following these basic tips, I would end up with basic results. Any success I had was obviously down to luck and when I failed, it was because I wasn't doing it correctly. I still really had no clue what I was doing. All my successes were achieved with plants such as pothos or *Tradescantia pallida* (purple-heart spiderwort). Now, if you know anything about propagating these plants, you'll know they start growing roots as soon as the blades of your shears separate them from the mother plant. Yes, I'm exaggerating, but they really do root quickly. Clearly, I still didn't know enough to cut confidently from the plants I owned and had grown to love. I needed more info.

These were the sorts of questions I had: Where is the best place on a plant to make a cut? Do you place the cutting in regular water right away or does the water have to sit overnight to de-chlorinate? Do you need to use hormone-rooting powder? Can you just stick the cutting directly into potting mix? If not, why not? How long does it take for a cutting to root? Once the cutting shows roots, is it then time to stick it in potting mix? I had so many questions and very few answers. So, like most of us, I ran to the Internet for help and advice. And, as most of you also know, that can be a world of mixed messages. So, who are you to trust?

I made a huge mistake a few years back when I was planning to move from New Orleans to Baltimore, and thought it would be nice to give my friend a cutting of Frank (my fiddle-leaf fig), so a part of him could live on there. I'd read that you simply make a sharp cut anywhere on a branch, dip the cutting in hormone-rooting powder, place it in water, and then wait. Well, I decided to give this approach a try. I cut off one of Frank's large branches and watched as each leaf attached to that branch slowly died. Not only had I made a mistake with the cutting, but was also unaware of the trauma I would cause Frank. A few days later, Frank lost a few more leaves, after not having lost any

OPPOSITE

This cutting of *Tradescantia pallida* (purple-heart spiderwort) started from a plant that was originally a cutting I was given in 2014. As the plant continued to grow, I'd cut it, place the new cutting in water, and continue the propagating process. I now have a fully grown plant that hangs in my bedroom window.

in the first year I had him. While I can't say for sure that cutting off one of his branches was the cause, I definitely know it didn't help. I never forgave myself and, as a result, have never tried to propagate Frank again. If I did, then at least I know how I'd go about it now. You see, learning about propagation, as with most of what I know about plants and their care, has come from trial and error. And because of this, so has successful propagation.

There are a few propagation techniques, including dividing plants and taking stem and tip cuttings, so first find out what type of plant you have so you can choose the right method. For example, for cuttings, you need to know exactly what kind of cut to make and where to make that cut (i.e. either along or at the tip of a stem or branch). The main propagation techniques are explained on the following pages. So, with that said, here is what you need to know to propagate your own plant buds.

Hoya carnosa

division

While some plants are propagated by taking cuttings, other plants need to be separated through division. This technique is used for plants like *Strelitzia reginae* (bird of paradise), ferns, palms, and a few succulents. Often, these plants come with multiple stems growing out of the pot, or will grow a new shoot once the plant has settled in and begun to thrive. At this stage, the pot can become overcrowded with roots and stems, and the best way to make sure the plant is happy is to divide it and replant it in two pots.

what you'll need

Mother plant (suitable for dividing)

Potting mix (to suit the type of plant)

2 pots

Drop cloth (dust sheet)

Gardening gloves

1   Make sure you have the proper potting mix and the right sized pots. Fill the base of the pots with potting mix, as you would when potting up a new plant (see page 101).

2   Lay out a drop cloth (dust sheet), so you can collect any excess potting mix and limit the mess you make. Pull the plant from its original pot and place it on top of the cloth.

3   Wearing gloves, start gently separating the roots of the plant. Depending on the type of plant, the roots could be fairly large or thin. Just take your time and pull them apart. Don't panic if you break a few, as they'll recover once the plant is repotted.

4   Take the first divided plant and place it in one of the pots. Hold the plant upright with one hand (or get a partner to help) and start scooping potting mix into the pot to cover the roots and the base of the plant. Once you have scooped in enough fresh potting mix, pat down gently and repeat the same steps for the other plant.

5   Once your plant is divided into two pots, place the plants in their new spots and water them in. Then follow the same watering routine as for the mother plant.

Sansevieria trifasciata

the stem cut

Stem cuttings are typically taken from plants that are more vine-like in shape and growth. Some of the plants featured in this book are propagated through stem cuttings. These include *Scindapsus pictus* 'Argyraeus' (satin pothos), various monsteras, *Philodendron* 'Burle Marx', *P. scandens* (heart-leaf philodendron), *Schlumbergera* (Christmas cactus), and *Maranta leuconeura* (prayer plant).

I've had most success with plants propagated by stem cuttings. I think this is because they have easy-to-find identifiers that show where to make a cut. And those easy identifiers are their nodes. Nodes are those little bumps along the vine of your pothos or the base of your monstera. They are basically baby roots waiting to be placed in water, so they can grow and produce more roots.

what you'll need

Mother plant (suitable for taking cuttings)
Sharp blade or hand pruners (secateurs)
Glass vessel
Water at room temperature
A little patience

1   Locate a healthy stem or branch on your plant. You'll want one that doesn't have dead or browning leaves. If it's green, it's a go!

2   Find the node along the plant's stem or branch. Remember these are the bumps below each leaf of the plant.

3   Take a sharp blade or hand pruners (secateurs) and cut 1 inch (2.5cm) below the node, making sure the stem you are cutting has two to three healthy leaves. The technique still works if you want to take a longer cutting, but it's crucial that the leaves and stem are healthy.

4   Fill the glass vessel with water at room temperature. This is necessary so you don't shock the cutting as it goes into the water. Imagine how you feel when you first jump into a cold pool. You want to avoid that for your cutting.

5   Place the cutting in the vessel, making sure the node closest to where the cut was made is completely and always submerged in water. The roots will develop from this node.

NOTE: On some plants, such as *Monstera deliciosa* (Swiss cheese plant), the plant's nodes become long aerial roots, looking to stretch out and wrap around trees or other plants in order to climb higher in the wild. So, if you locate one of these aerial roots on your indoor plant, cut it down to a nub, make your cut below that, and then place the cutting in water.

the tip cut

Tip cuttings are exactly that—you're going to be making cuts from the tip of the plant's branches. In most cases, you make the cut where the tip is still green. The plants featured in this book that can be propagated by taking tip cuttings are *Ficus lyrata* (fiddle-leaf fig), *F. elastica* (rubber plant), *Sansevieria trifasciata* (snake plant), *Zamioculcas zamiifolia* (fern arum/ZZ plant), *Dracaena*, and *Crassula ovata* (money tree).

what you'll need

> Mother plant (suitable for taking cuttings)
>
> Sharp blade or hand pruners (secateurs)
>
> Glass vessel
> Water at room temperature
> A little patience

1   Locate a healthy stem or branch on your plant. You'll want a stem that doesn't have dead or browning leaves. If the stem is green, then great, but this is especially important with plants such as the fiddle-leaf fig (shown here), rubber plant, and money plant. For these plants, find the green area of the branch. If you look from the trunk of the plant to the tip of new growth, you'll notice a change in coloration and texture. At the trunk, the surface of the plant looks more "tree-like" (i.e. like bark). But, as you make your way to the tip, you'll find an area that's new and green. That's where you need to make your cut.

2   Take a sharp blade or hand pruners (secateurs) and cut 2 inches (5cm) below the last leaf, making sure the cut is at a 45-degree angle. The angle is important because it creates the most surface area for rooting to take place. The larger the cut area, the more likely it is that you'll propagate your plant successfully.

3   With a snake plant, like most succulents or cacti, you can make the cut anywhere, although a 45-degree angle cut is also recommended for these plants. If done correctly, you'll see multiple new shoots growing from the one cutting.

4   As for stem cuttings, fill the glass vessel with water, checking that this is at room temperature.

5   Place the cutting in the vessel, ensuring the area where the cut was made is completely and always submerged in water. The roots will develop from this cut.

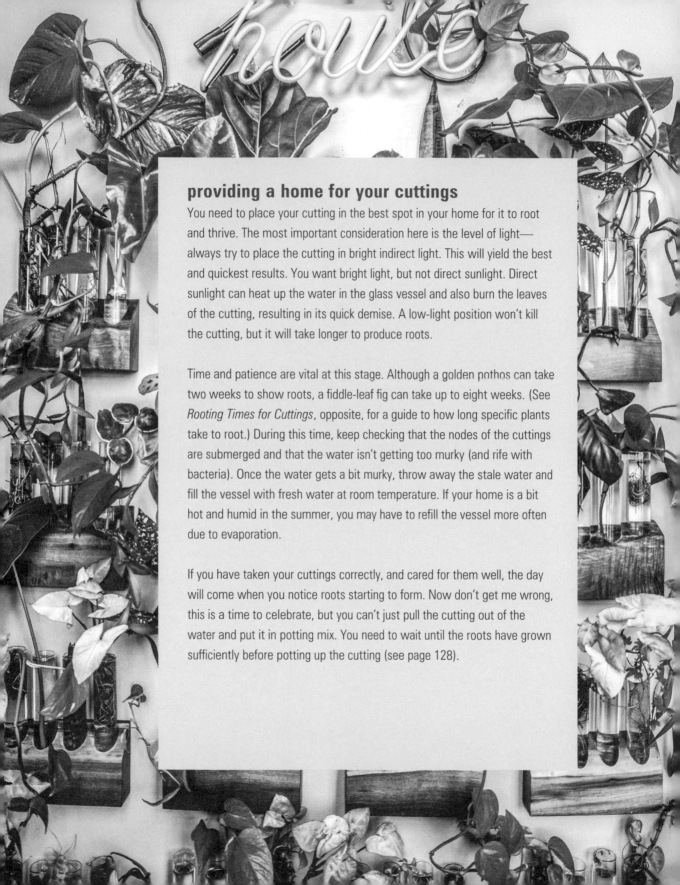

providing a home for your cuttings

You need to place your cutting in the best spot in your home for it to root and thrive. The most important consideration here is the level of light—always try to place the cutting in bright indirect light. This will yield the best and quickest results. You want bright light, but not direct sunlight. Direct sunlight can heat up the water in the glass vessel and also burn the leaves of the cutting, resulting in its quick demise. A low-light position won't kill the cutting, but it will take longer to produce roots.

Time and patience are vital at this stage. Although a golden pothos can take two weeks to show roots, a fiddle-leaf fig can take up to eight weeks. (See *Rooting Times for Cuttings*, opposite, for a guide to how long specific plants take to root.) During this time, keep checking that the nodes of the cuttings are submerged and that the water isn't getting too murky (and rife with bacteria). Once the water gets a bit murky, throw away the stale water and fill the vessel with fresh water at room temperature. If your home is a bit hot and humid in the summer, you may have to refill the vessel more often due to evaporation.

If you have taken your cuttings correctly, and cared for them well, the day will come when you notice roots starting to form. Now don't get me wrong, this is a time to celebrate, but you can't just pull the cutting out of the water and put it in potting mix. You need to wait until the roots have grown sufficiently before potting up the cutting (see page 128).

Sansevieria trifasciata

Ficus elastica

ROOTING TIMES FOR CUTTINGS

Propagating in water is one of my favorite ways to increase my plant family. The time it takes for cuttings to show roots varies depending on the type of plant and the light it's getting. So, stay patient and have fun! Below are the estimated times for a selection of cuttings to show roots:

Aglaonema (Chinese evergreen)...3 weeks

Crassula ovata (money tree)...3 weeks

Ficus elastica (rubber plant)..8 weeks

Ficus lyrata (fiddle-leaf fig)...6–8 weeks

Ficus pumila (creeping fig)...1 week

Hoya carnosa (wax plant)...2 weeks

Monstera standleyana ....2–3 weeks

Philodendron 'Burle Marx' ....1 week

Philodendron scandens (heart-leaf philodendron) ....1 week

Tradescantia pallida (purple-heart spiderwort) ....1 week

Sansevieria trifasciata (snake plant) ....4 weeks

Schlumbergera (Christmas cactus)...2 weeks

Scindapsus pictus 'Argyraeus' (satin pothos)..................................1 week

Zamioculcas zamiifolia (fern arum/ZZ plant)..................................4 weeks

Ficus pumila

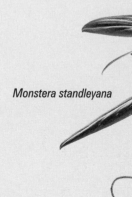

Monstera standleyana

from water to soil—potting up your cuttings

Many people think that propagation has been successful when they see a cutting forming roots or a new shoot, but, for me, it isn't a success until you've potted up the cutting and it is thriving. So, before potting up your cutting, ensure it has sufficiently long roots or you can see a new shoot starting to grow.

what you'll need

Right size pot (for your cutting)
Fresh potting mix
Small gardening spade or spoon
Gardening gloves
Small piece of wood and some string or Velcro, for staking (optional)

1   You need a pot that is just the right size for your cutting. To gauge this, use the following as a guide: for every ½ inch (1cm) that your cutting is in diameter, the circumference of the pot needs to be 10 times that. For example, if a fiddle-leaf fig stem is ½ inch (1cm) wide, you need a pot with a diameter of 5 inches (13cm).

2   Start scooping potting mix into the bottom of the pot until it's almost filled to the top.

3   Use your hands to create a little hole in the center of the potting mix, about 2–3 inches (5–7.5cm) down. Pull the cutting from its glass vessel and place carefully in the little planting hole.

4   Cover the roots and the base of the stem with potting mix (**4a**), adding more as needed.

5   Gently pat down the top of the potting mix, making sure the cutting is secure in its new home.

6   If the cutting is too heavy to stand upright on its own, make a stake out of a small piece of wood and press this into the potting mix. Then take a short length of string or piece of Velcro and tie the cutting to the stake to provide extra support. Once the roots of the cutting have grown longer and are strong, and the cutting can support its own weight, you can remove the stake.

7   Water your cutting. Then follow the same watering routine as the mother plant from which you took the cutting.

8   If you do all this correctly, you'll begin to see new growth in no time. And with that, you'll have a successful propagation and a new member of your plant family.

| 4 | 4a |

| 8 |

TROUBLESHOOTING

OPPOSITE
A yellowing leaf from our monstera.
Even in death there can still be beauty.

DISCOLORED/DROPPING LEAVES There could be many reasons why the foliage of your plant is losing its color and turning brown or yellow, including over- or under-watering and insufficient light. These changes in color are a sure sign of an unhealthy plant. Sometimes you may also see a plant dropping its leaves. But don't panic just yet, as the issue can usually be resolved—you just need to identify the exact cause and act accordingly. A plant may drop leaves, for example, just because it is maturing and shedding old growth in order to produce new growth. If you think this is the case with your plant, the only solution is to repot it in a larger pot. Leaves turning yellow is due to overwatering, so let the plant's potting mix dry out completely before the next watering and start paying attention to how much you're giving. If the plant's tips are turning brown, just make sure you're watering enough—until you see water coming out of the drainage hole of the pot.

The healthier a plant, the deeper and more vibrant the colors of the leaves will be. However, the color can vary depending on the exposure to light. Some plants, such as *Tradescantia pallida* (purple-heart spiderwort), are a deep violet when exposed to direct sunlight, but the foliage turns green in a spot with medium to low light.

DROOPING LEAVES When your plant's leaves start drooping or "fainting," this is an S.O.S. message to tell you that it needs water and needs it soon. These call-outs are like gold to a plant parent. The foliage of *Spathiphyllum*

wallisii (peace lily), for example, will faint when the plant is thirsty and will perk back up once given water. Similarly, the leaves of *Stromanthe sanguinea* 'Triostar' will curl up when it needs a drink and unfurl once satisfied. Plants that tell you when they need something are always welcome in my home. If you see drooping leaves on your plants, act with urgency and give your green friends some water. They'll thank you by perking up and showing off their vibrant colors once more.

WILTING This can happen when a plant is kept in a space with an unsuitable temperature. That could be by a heat vent or up against a cold window. Once you notice this, move the plant to a new spot and feel free to prune back the wilted leaves.

SUNBURN No one likes getting sunburnt. That's why we protect ourselves when exposed to excessive sun. When exposed to the heat of direct sun, the leaves of some plants are likely to become sunburnt—so they need the same protection. Signs of sunburn are brown spots on the foliage, as is the case for an under-watered plant. But the appearance of a sunburnt leaf, an under-watered one, or one that isn't receiving enough light differs. Sunburnt leaves have lighter brown spots with yellowish spots around them, and these look more like a burn. To prevent sunburn, move the plant away from the window or use a sheer drape (curtain) to filter any direct sun so it does not damage your plant friends.

PEST CONTROL

maintaining your plant gang means spending a lot of time watering, cleaning the leaves, rotating pots, and so on. Getting in there among your green buds really helps you feel as if you're a part of their lives. It also helps you notice when you may have a bug problem. When you first decided to bring the outside in, or create an indoor jungle, you thought that would include all the greenery, but not the bugs, right? I get that. But bugs are a part of the natural world, and so checking for bugs on your plants before they get out of control and kill your precious specimens is important.

Some of the most common houseplant pests include spider mites, mealy bugs (white and cotton-ball-like), insect scales, and gnats. You might not be able to see them from a distance, so getting right up in the foliage of your plants is the best way to identify the problem. Make sure you check above and below each leaf and around the potting mix. Once you notice a bug, take action immediately by separating the plant from others and using a proprietary pest-killing treatment, whether this is store-bought or homemade. While some people have success with organic neem oil insecticide, I prefer to use a simple homemade remedy composed of everyday household items that are harmful to the pests, but not to your plants.

making a bug remedy

The following steps for treating your plants with my homemade bug remedy should be repeated once a week for at least three weeks, to ensure the problem is resolved. I like to place my affected plant away from other plants while the treatment is taking effect. Yes, plant quarantine.

what you'll need

Measuring spoons or a teaspoon
1 teaspoon rubbing alcohol (surgical spirit)
1 teaspoon dish soap (washing-up liquid)
Plastic spray bottle with 1 cup (250ml) of water
Damp and dry cloths
Q-tips (cotton buds)

| 2 | 3 | 4 | 5 | 6 | 8 |

1 Take the plant to the sink, bathtub, or wherever is suitable for getting the foliage wet.

2 Carefully measure a teaspoon of rubbing alcohol (surgical spirit) and a teaspoon of dish soap (washing-up liquid) into a spray bottle filled with 1 cup (250ml) water.

3 Put the nozzle firmly back on the spray bottle and shake well.

4 Locate the bugs on the plant and spray the area generously with the bug remedy.

5 Let the plant sit for about 30 minutes. While the remedy is working on the plant, dump out the solution and fill the spray bottle with fresh water.

6 After 30 minutes, spray the plant with the fresh water. If you're able to take the plant outdoors and spray it with a garden hose, then do so—the more pressure behind the spray here, the better.

7 Take the damp cloth and wipe down the foliage of the plant. This will help clear off any lingering dead bugs, but also remove dust from the leaves. Use the dry cloth to dry off the plant, or just let it air-dry.

8 If you see just a few bugs from time to time, then dipping a q-tip (cotton bud) in some rubbing alcohol (surgical spirit) and spot-removing the bugs works well.

HILTON'S RECOMMENDED PLANTS

ALOCASIA
Elephant's ear

The *Alocasia* genus includes some insanely beautiful tropical plants, which, if placed in the right setting, can produce one of the most interesting and exotic flowers you'll ever see between the dark glossy leaves. Having said that, alocasias are among the hardest plants I've had to care for because they prefer to be kept moist, which means frequent watering. As a result, being self-aware when it comes to plants that require this level of care, I limit the number of specimens I have in my home and studio.

LIGHT Bright light or direct sunlight for most of the day. The better the light, the more the plant will thrive and the larger the leaves will be. The more direct sun alocasias receive, the more you'll probably have to water them.

TEMPERATURE Although alocasias like warm temperatures, it's best to keep them in a space that's 60–80°F (15–27°C) during the day and no colder than 60°F (15°C) at night.

WATERING Water often to ensure the potting mix is kept moist, but do not submerge in water or allow to become waterlogged, as this can cause root rot. To keep humidity levels good during the drier months, mist every few days.

REPOTTING Repot in spring or summer for the best results. Make sure the new pot is at least 2 inches (5cm) larger than the previous one.

PROPAGATION Divide in spring (see *Division*, pages 120–121).

CRASSULA OVATA
Money tree, friendship tree

I find that the money tree—which is thought to bring its owner wealth—makes a nice addition to an indoor jungle because it doesn't require a ton of light and also grows quite slowly. This means you don't have to repot it or move it to a new location very often. Although you can place a money tree in low-light areas, they thrive best in bright indirect light.

LIGHT Low to medium light. I've had most success when a money tree is placed in a bright window that gets direct sun in the morning and six to eight hours of bright light per day. They can still, however, tolerate low-light situations.

TEMPERATURE Try keeping money trees in a space that's 65–80°F (18–27°C) during the day and no colder than 60°F (15°C) at night.

WATERING Water when the top 2 inches (5cm) of potting mix is dry to the touch. Water slowly to ensure the potting mix is evenly hydrated and until you see water coming out of the drainage hole. Discard the excess water.

REPOTTING Repot in spring or summer for the best results. Make sure the new pot

FICUS ELASTICA
Rubber plant

A rubber plant has been the perfect addition to my collection. This thick-leaved tropical beauty is very durable in high-traffic areas, while its deep green/purple hue rings in the changes nicely among other greenery. In the right setting these tree-like plants grow fairly quickly and can reach up to 25 feet (7.6m), so prune when necessary or be prepared to poke a hole in your ceiling! I selfishly prefer the latter. A rubber plant was my third or fourth plant purchse and grew so fast that I was encouraged to see I was doing something right. I've since bought four more rubber plants, two of which are variegated. I know monsteras and fiddle-leaf figs have been all the rage in recent years, but I'm calling it here right now: the rubber plant will be the next trend-setting plant. Book it!

LIGHT Bright indirect light to direct sun. I've had most success when a rubber plant is placed in a bright window that gets direct sun in the morning and six to eight hours of bright light per day.

TEMPERATURE Given that the rubber plant is native to the jungle and tropical climates, it is best kept in a space that's 65–80°F (18–27°C) during the day and no colder than 60°F (15°C) at night.

is at least 2 inches (5cm) larger than the previous one.

PROPAGATION Tip cuttings in spring (see *The Tip Cut*, pages 124–125).

WATER Rubber plants prefer to get completely dry before being given a drink, so only water when the top 2 inches (5cm) of potting mix is dry to the touch. Water slowly to ensure the potting mix is evenly hydrated and until you see water coming out of the drainage hole. Discard the exess water.

REPOTTING Repot in spring or summer for the best results. Make sure the new pot is at least 2 inches (5cm) larger than the previous one.

PROPAGATION Tip cuttings in spring or summer (see *The Tip Cut*, pages 124–125).

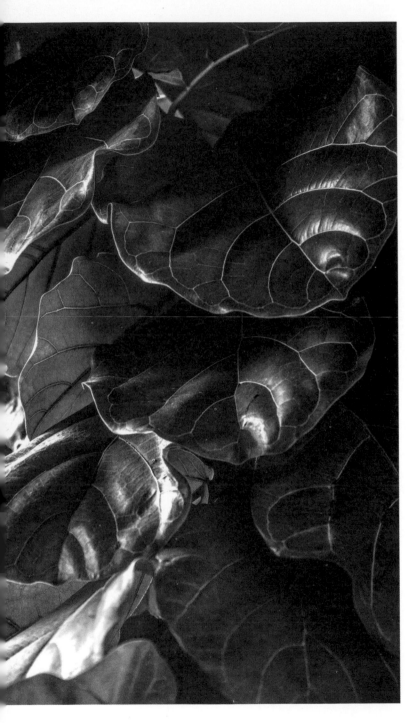

Fiddle-leaf fig

You already know how fond I am of the fiddle-leaf fig—so much so that today I care for four in total: Frank, Treezus, Clavel, and Lil' Baby. Yeah that's right! I name my plants and so should you. But be aware that you'll need to do a lot to care well for a fiddle-leaf fig. Regarded by many as the most finicky plant you can have in a plant collection, it will be a challenge out of the gate. But you just need the right tools and tips to keep you on your toes and your head in the game—good thing I have all those right here for you. You can thank me later.

LIGHT Placing a fiddle-leaf fig in a spot that gets bright indirect light is everything. If a fiddle is ever going to get direct sunlight, it's best that it is early morning sun rather than bright afternoon sun. Hard sun will burn the leaves, creating yellowish and brown spots that look different to the brown spots you get as a result of under-watering, or the yellowing of leaves that occurs after overwatering. Basically, the brighter the indirect light, the better. Plants that don't do well up against a southwest-facing window will tell you over time and eventually die. So please be aware of that.

TEMPERATURE This jungle buddy likes it warm, to mimic its native habitat. Keep fiddles in a space that's 65–80°F (18–27°C) during the day and no colder than 60°F (15°C) at night.

WATERING Only water when the top 2 inches (5cm) of potting mix is completely dry. Once I know my fiddles are dry, I water them with an exact amount each time. I base how much water they need on how much water drains into the base tray. Once the water has drained completely into the tray, I wait an hour and then either lift the plant to the side and discard the water or take a towel and wrap it around the base of the pot to soak up the water. Don't let your plant sit in water for days, as this will cause root rot over time and, again, eventually kill your plant.

REPOTTING Repot in spring or summer for the best results. Make sure the new pot is at least 2 inches (5cm) larger than the previous one. Remember, a fiddle hates to be moved, so once you've found a good spot, keep it there. Don't panic just because it loses a leaf or two and then move it to another window. That'll only prolong the trauma.

ROTATION Rotate your fiddle every two months or so. I noticed at some point with Frank that the branches closest to the window grew new leaves most consistently. So I started to let one branch get its time in the bright part of the window. Once that branch had developed new leaves, I'd rotate a new branch into that part of the window, and repeat the process. So, it's important to rotate your fiddle to ensure balanced growth.

PROPAGATION Tip cuttings in spring or summer (see *The Tip Cut*, pages 124–125).

MONSTERA DELICIOSA
Swiss cheese plant

This large leaved plant is used to climbing trees in its natural habitat, so giving it room and helping it grow upward will stop it spreading out along the floor. It will also take any space to the next level in terms of styling. In the wild, the monstera's large foliage naturally splits to give the lower leaves a better chance of receiving light. So, the better the light, the more splits and holes the foliage will have. That's why the monstera is also known as the Swiss cheese plant. The air roots that help monsteras to climb trees develop with the plant, but can be left to grow outside the pot indoors. If you wish, just remove these air roots with sharp shears or hand pruners (secateurs).

LIGHT Medium to bright indirect light. In nature you'll see monsteras growing up trees, mostly shaded from direct sun. I've had most success when a Swiss cheese plant is placed in a bright window that gets direct sun in the morning and six to eight hours of bright light per day.

TEMPERATURE Given this is a tropical plant used to warm climates, recreating this type of environment will produce the best results. Keep monsteras in a space that's 65–75°F (18–24°C) during the day and no colder than 60°F (15°C) at night.

WATERING Water when the top 2 inches (5cm) of potting mix is dry to the touch. Water slowly to ensure the potting mix is

evenly hydrated and until you see water coming out of the drainage hole. Discard the excess water.

REPOTTING Repot in spring or summer for the best results. Make sure the new pot is at least 2 inches (5cm) larger than the previous one.

PROPAGATION Stem cuttings in spring (see *The Stem Cut*, pages 122–123).

NEPHROLEPIS BISERRATA 'MACHO'
Macho fern

The macho fern is exactly that, macho. Appropriately named, given its big burly stature, this fern makes its cousin, *Nephrolepis exaltata* (Boston fern), look small. My love for ferns started when I first saw them hanging from the balconies in the French Quarter of New Orleans. Large and eye-catching, they have a unique way of instantly making any space feel more lush and vibrant. With their long, deep green fronds and bushy frame, you'll find yourself quickly drawn. However, unlike the other plants in my collection, the ferns ask for more attention. So, knowing this, I limit the number of ferns I have to avoid getting overwhelmed and neglecting my plants.

LIGHT Medium to bright light for most of the day. Avoid placing in areas that get direct sunlight.

TEMPERATURE Keep macho ferns in a space that's 65–78°F (18–26°C) during the day and no colder than 60°F (15°C) at night.

WATERING Keeping a fern alive and thriving depends on how often you water it—ensuring the potting mix is kept moist is key. Depending on the fern's position in your home, you may have to water it every four to six days.

REPOTTING Repot in spring or summer for the best results. Make sure the new pot is at least 2 inches (5cm) larger than the previous one.

PROPAGATION Divide in spring (see *Division*, pages 120–121).

SANSEVIERIA TRIFASCIATA
Snake plant

The snake plant clearly derives one of its common names from the scale-like pattern of the leaves, but I bet it also has something to do with its curling/bending shape. It is considered by most plant enthusiasts to be a "hard-to-kill" plant. Early on in my plant-caring career, I found it not so "hard to kill." You see, when you're a new plant parent, you tend to smother your plants, just like any new parent. In my case, it was with too much water. I soon learnt my lesson, however, and continue to bring snake plants into my home. What I absolutely love about the snake plant is that, unlike other desert plants, it can be tucked into low-light spots, making it easier to spread the plant love throughout your living space, even when you don't have many windows. When you have over 300 plants to care for, you want to share the duties with others. Well, that's where my wife comes in. Her job is to handle all the snakes in our home. We call it, "snake patrol."

LIGHT Perfect for the space that doesn't get much light, but also perfect for the one that does. That's the best part about the snake plant. While snake plants will thrive and quickly grow tall in bright light, they will still thrive in low light. The only difference is that the growth will be much slower.

TEMPERATURE Given that the snake plant is native to desert climates, it's best kept in a space that's 65–80°F (18–27°C) during the day and no colder than 50°F (10°C) at night.

WATERING Kin to the cactus, the snake plant likes to dry out and go without water for a few weeks between each watering. Overwatering is the main reason most people kill this plant. So be stingy when giving this plant bud a drink. I've found it works to place my snake plants and other cacti on the same schedule and only water them every two to three weeks.

REPOTTING Repot in spring or summer for the best results. Make sure the new pot is at least 2 inches (5cm) larger than the previous one.

PROPAGATION Tip cuttings in spring or summer (see *The Tip Cut*, pages 124–125).

SPATHIPHYLLUM WALLISII
Peace lily

This tropical beauty is one of my favorite plants, not only because it is low-maintenance, but also because in the right setting it produces these beautiful, tear-drop-like flowers. While peace lilies allow you to get away with placing them in low-light areas, they live their best lives in bright indirect light. Helpfully, this plant will "tell" you when it needs watering because the large, dark green leaves fall in a fainting position. To the newbie, this might seem as if your plant is dying on you. But rest assured, once you water your peace lily, the leaves will perk back up as if served their first cup of morning coffee.

LIGHT Low, medium, or bright light for most of the day. The better the light, the more flowers your plant will produce and the larger those flowers will be.

TEMPERATURE Try to keep peace lilies in a space that's 65–78°F (18–26°C) during the day and no colder than 60°F (15°C) at night.

WATERING Only water when the potting mix is dry to the touch or when the leaves are drooping low—this is a sure sign that your peace lily is ready for a drink.

REPOTTING Repot in spring or summer for the best results. Make sure the new pot is at least 2 inches (5cm) larger than the previous one.

PROPAGATION Divide in spring (see *Division*, pages 120–121).

STRELITZIA REGINAE
Bird of paradise

This large-leaved tropical plant is perfectly named after the beautiful, bird-like flowers it produces in the right environment. And, in most cases, that environment is outdoors or in a greenhouse. It is difficult to get a bird of paradise to flower in the average home, so if you're able to, put this book down and give yourself a pat on the back. I love how large the paddle-like leaves of this plant get and how it can instantly bring a "jungle" feel to any space. The bird of paradise can grow large in the right setting, so make sure you have enough room. Another thing I love about this plant is that it's fairly easy to care for if you're giving it all the things it needs.

LIGHT Bright indirect light to direct sun. I've had most success when a bird of paradise is placed in a bright window that gets direct sun in the morning and six to eight hours of bright light per day.

TEMPERATURE Given this is a tropical plant used to warm climates, recreating this type of environment produces the best results. Keep birds of paradise in a space that's 65–75°F (18–24°C) during the day and no colder than 55°F (13°C) at night.

WATERING Water when the top 2 inches (5cm) of potting mix is dry to the touch. Water slowly to ensure the potting mix is evenly hydrated and until you see water coming out of the drainage hole. Discard the excess water.

REPOTTING Repot in spring or summer for the best results. Make sure the new pot is at least 2 inches (5cm) larger than the previous one.

PROPAGATION Divide in spring (see *Division*, pages 120–121).

STROMANTHE SANGUINEA 'Triostar'

Often simply referred to as a triostar, this is such an amazing plant for your styled home. With its beautifully variegated pink, green, and cream foliage, it can grow up to 3 feet (10m) tall, with a bush-like shape similar to that of a peace lily. What makes the triostar really cool is that, unlike most plants, it will curl up its leaves to indicate when it's thirsty. Water straightaway when you see this happen—if left without water for too long, the leaf tips turn brown.

LIGHT Medium light. I've had most success when a triostar is placed in a window that receives bright indirect light, but because of this, you'll probably have to water more frequently. Make sure to keep out of direct sun.

TEMPERATURE Keep triostars in a space that's 65–75°F (18–24°C) during the day and no colder than 60°F (15°C) at night.

WATERING Water often to keep the potting mix moist. Although triostars need to be kept moist, do not submerge in water or allow to become waterlogged, as this can cause root rot. They love humidity, so mist during the drier months.

REPOTTING Repot in spring or summer for the best results. Make sure the new pot is at least 2 inches (5cm) larger than the previous one.

PROPAGATION Divide in spring (see *Division*, pages 120–121).

index

LOVE AND THANKS

This book is dedicated to my wife, Fiona. You are the true architect of my happiness and the reason any of this has been possible. Without your boundless love, patience, and selfless support, I couldn't have achieved this dream. I love you.

Thank you to my mother, Tracy, for encouraging me to create as a kid. Who would have thought that would mean creating a book on plant styling? Thanks to the many friends and family that have supported me in the process. Thank you to my brother, Aaron Keeny, for the additional support with the photography. We've worked together for over 20 years and I couldn't imagine making this without you on my team.

Thank you to all of the friends that opened their homes to me so I could style their spaces and photograph them for this book. To Jamie and Drury, thanks for letting me help create in your space and for giving me so much time and space to do so. To Elan and Brenna, thanks for sharing your home, time, and love. Your support through this process was so appreciated. Thanks to Jessica and Michael for letting me play in your space so that I could make your family room something special. Thanks to Michelle for inspiring me to get a home with a screened-in porch. I see how necessary that is now.

To Patty Wilson, thank you for planting the seed in me to propagate and for the early encouragement when

I first got into greenery. Your generosity and love will never be forgotten. Thank you to Justina Blakeney, Grace Bonney, and the wonderful folks at Apartment Therapy for their kind and encouraging words. Justina, thank you for being a force in the styling industry and for inspiring me daily. Grace, thanks for always being real and showing us all how to do so as well. And Apartment Therapy, thank you for letting me share with you and for bringing me in as family. I've been inspired by the content that all three of you share and in many ways it's the reason why this book exists.

Thank you to Jennifer Nolley and David Tufaro for their support. I couldn't have made Jungle by the Falls come together if it wasn't for you both. Thanks to Terrain for inspiring me to first bring plants into my home. Your garden café changed my life.

Thank you to everyone at CICO who helped make this book happen, especially Anna, Caroline, and Cindy. I'm so thankful for this collaboration and the time you all put into making this book what it is. Thank you.

Lastly, thank you, my green-loving community. We share in this together. This book is for us. I truly hope you find something that you can pull from the book and apply to your own homes, or that helps you provide that extra care for your green friends.

Thank you.